Trinity

Union St.

Lower Brook St.

Lawn St.

Eastgate St.

Water

Beggar's La

St John's St.

Morn Hill

Tunnel Road

St. John's Ch.

Street

Guildhall

Abbey Grounds

Soke Bridge

Bridge St.

Cheesehill St.

Great Western Sta.

...brook St.

Castle

Wolvesey Palace

College

Road

...ine's Rd

A
WINCHESTER MISCELLANY

A WINCHESTER MISCELLANY

Summersdale Publishers Ltd
46 West Street
Chichester
West Sussex
PO19 1RP
UK

www.summersdale.com

Printed and bound by CPI Group (UK) Ltd, Croydon, CR0 4YY

ISBN: 978-1-84953-464-2

Substantial discounts on bulk quantities of Summersdale books are available to corporations, professional associations and other organisations. For details contact Nicky Douglas by telephone: +44 (0) 1243 756902, fax: +44 (0) 1243 786300 or email: nicky@summersdale.com.

A
WINCHESTER MISCELLANY

PHIL HEWITT

summersdale

WINCHESTER

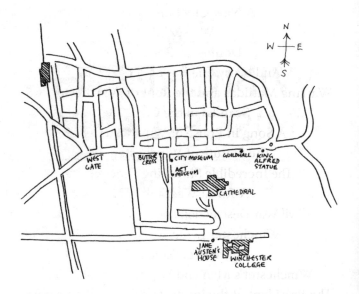

WEST GATE

BUTTER CROSS

CITY MUSEUM

ACT MUSEUM

GUILDHALL

KING ALFRED STATUE

CATHEDRAL

JANE AUSTEN'S HOUSE

WINCHESTER COLLEGE

N
W E
S

CONTENTS

Winchester Places

Winchester People

Winchester Culture

INTRODUCTION

Welcome to Winchester

*Apart indeed from the metropolis, there is
no city in the land about which so many
memories linger and so many wonderful
historical associations are centred as
Winchester. Here our history seems veritably
to be a living reality.*

BEAUTIFUL BRITAIN: WINCHESTER, REVD TELFORD-
VARLEY, (ADAM & CHARLES BLACK, 1914)

Winchester is a city of irresistible majesty and romance;
a place where myth meets legend, and where both are
deliciously surpassed by a truth stranger than fiction.

Thirty-five kings made Winchester their capital;
twenty kings are buried in its cathedral – a remarkable
statistic which underlines just how much, and for
how long, the history of Winchester was the history
of England.

Winchester is a place where kings and queens were born, married, lived and died; a place where a cake-burning king established a nation, and where William the Conqueror built a mighty castle. It was also the city where a despised dead king was unceremoniously dumped in a cart; and the city to which another king hastened simply so that he could tell the world that his first-born was born in Winchester.

Just as fascinating as the history are the legends. Winchester is a place where fact and fancy collide, a city where you can enjoy history and mystery in almost equal measure.

To appreciate Winchester is to appreciate the extravagance of the stories it tells. As Charles Ball noted two centuries ago in his *Historical Account of Winchester* (1818), Winchester is a city 'enveloped by the mist of uncertainty and romance which characterises the early History of our Island'.

The stories are irresistible: the tale of the maligned queen who walked on red-hot ploughshares to prove that she wasn't cavorting with the bishop; the legend of the annoyed saint who conjured forty days and nights of rain when his body was moved after his death; the tale of the nobleman who continued to recite the Lord's Prayer even after the executioner's sword had fallen...

And who knows, it may well have been in Winchester that King Arthur ruled his Camelot.

But certainly true is the remarkable story of the courageous deep-sea diver who single-handedly saved the city's 900-year-old cathedral, shoring up its crumbling foundations in its hour of need, a century ago.

Winchester is a city for people who love this country's heritage; it is also the place for those of us who love a good yarn.

Come with me now as we take a look at **Winchester Times**, at **Winchester Places**, at **Winchester Culture** and at **Winchester People**. A fascinating journey lies ahead.

Phil Hewitt
September 2013

OVERVIEW

The county town of Hampshire, Winchester is roughly 70 miles south-west of London, 14 miles north-east of Southampton and 25 miles north-west of Portsmouth. It is linked to the world by the A31, the A34 and the M3 close by.

Situated on the River Itchen and the hillside above it, Winchester finds itself at the western end of the South Downs range of chalk hills along which snakes the South Downs Way, a much-loved route which takes the walker along some of the finest countryside in the south of England. Starting at the white chalk cliffs of Beachy Head, near Eastbourne, the South Downs Way follows 100 miles of ridges, ancient routes and droveways along the chalk escarpment. The reward at the end is a splendid view of Winchester and the water meadows in the Itchen valley beside it.

Approaching the city from the south is the Itchen Navigation, the modified river and former canal which runs from Wharf Bridge in Winchester to Woodmill in Southampton, stretching just over ten miles. With footpaths along its entire length, it exploits – just like the South Downs Way – the natural advantages which make Winchester's setting so special.

As the farmer and journalist William Cobbett noted nearly two centuries ago:

> *This vale of Itchen is worthy of particular attention. There are few spots in England more fertile or more pleasant; and none, I believe, more healthy [...] When we consider these things we are not surprised that a spot, situated about half way down this vale should have been chosen for the building of a city, or that that city should have been for a great number of years a place of residence for the Kings of England.*
>
> RURAL RIDES, WILLIAM COBBETT (1830)

As with most places of significance, Winchester has gone through a number of names with changing times. It was successively: Wenta (British); Caer Gwent (Celtic); Venta Belgarum (Roman); Wintan ceastre (ninth century); Winteceastre (tenth century); and Wyncestre (thirteenth century) before becoming Winchester. You can also find: Ouenta (*c.*150), Uintancæstir (*c.*730) and Wincestre (1086). Venta became Uin and Win, and a possible meaning is 'loved place'. Chester means simply 'city or walled town'.

Home to Hampshire County Council and to Winchester City Council, the city boasts a population of around 42,000.

King Arthur

Few figures come more beguilingly wrapped in myth and romance than **Arthur**; and Winchester just might have been his Camelot.

Tradition makes Arthur King of Britain; history says he was more likely a fifth- or sixth-century Romano-British chieftain or general. Our fascination with this shadowy figure is precisely because Arthur is the point where history meets with folklore and where fact swirls with legend to produce some of the most stirring tales our nation has ever told – stories of chivalry and charm, strong in colour and rich in passion.

Arthur, his love life, his knights, their infighting and their quest for the Holy Grail have inspired countless writers, dramatists and poets down the centuries, plus numerous film-makers in more recent times. The myth of Arthur is one that our country returns to time and time again.

Arthur is referred to in the British poem *The Gododdin* (*c*.600), placing him in the immediate post-Roman period, but for the Arthur we know, it's Geoffrey of Monmouth (*c*.1100–*c*.1155) we have to thank, with his fictional *Historia Regum Britanniae* (*History of the Kings of Britain*). Geoffrey gave us the wizard Merlin, Arthur's wife Guinevere and the sword Excalibur. The French writer Chrétien de Troyes then added Lancelot and the quest for the Holy Grail in the 1170s and 1180s. Between them, they created much of the Arthurian world we know today, offering the basis for the verse and prose romances that followed in the age of chivalry.

Edward I, who reigned from 1272 to 1307, was happy to encourage the legends, as were his successors. However, it was perhaps Sir Thomas Malory who did the most to keep the story alive when he retold it as a tragedy, printed in 1485 by Caxton as *Le Morte Darthur*.

First mentioned in Arthurian literature in 1115, a key element in Arthurian romance is Arthur's celebrated **Round Table**, a piece of pre-Conquest egalitarianism which enabled the knights to be seated in such a way that none had precedence. Winchester has got a round table; for many, it's confirmation enough that Winchester – just as Malory believed – was indeed Camelot, seat of Arthur's court.

Winchester's Round Table has in fact been dated back to the mid to late thirteenth century. Edward I and his queen visited Glastonbury in 1278 to see what were said to be the bones of Arthur and Guinevere; the chances are that Winchester's Round Table was created not long afterwards, to celebrate the betrothal of one of Edward I's daughters. Dendrochronological and radiocarbon dating, carried out in 1976, suggests a date range for the table between 1250 and 1280, which would fit with Edward being its instigator.

Measuring six metres across and made of oak, it is displayed in the Great Hall of Winchester Castle and bears a design painted on the orders of Henry VIII in 1522, with Henry himself the model for its depiction of Arthur. In the middle is a Tudor rose. The central inscription reads: 'This is the rownde table of kynge Arthur w[ith] xxiiii of hys namyde knyttes'.

Winchester's place at the heart of Arthurian romance was underlined once again in June 1934 when headmaster **W. F. Oakeshott** made the most remarkable of discoveries in the library of Winchester College. Oakeshott was cataloguing manuscripts when he came upon a previously unknown copy of Thomas Malory's *Le Morte Darthur* – a manuscript without printer Caxton's division into 21 books or Caxton's addition of chapter summaries. Instead, it divided the whole into eight parts, the basis for an important new edition of Malory, in effect Malory without Caxton's revisions.

Other Winchesters around the World

There is a Winchester in Canada; there is also a Winchester in New Zealand; but the United States of America has proved comfortably the most enthusiastic adopter of the great Winchester name. Half the states have one: namely Arkansas, California, Connecticut, Georgia, Idaho, Illinois, Indiana, Iowa, Kansas, Kentucky, Maryland, Massachusetts, Mississippi, Missouri, Nevada, New Hampshire, New York, Ohio, Oklahoma, Oregon, Tennessee, Texas, Virginia, Washington, Wisconsin and Wyoming.

A New City Emerges

Earliest settlement in the Winchester area dates back to prehistoric times, with three Iron Age hill forts, now known as Oram's Arbour, St Catherine's Hill and Worthy Down. And then our cousins on the other side of the Channel took a hand in Winchester's development. The Belgae – a name given to them by the Romans – were an ancient Celtic people who lived in Gaul north of the Seine and Marne rivers. Some of them crossed to southern England where they set up kingdoms at modern-day Silchester and Winchester. At first Winchester was eclipsed by Silchester to the north, but steadily Winchester grew, becoming the capital of the local Belgae.

The town took its next major leap forward with the arrival of the Romans who gave it the name **Venta Belgarum**, meaning either market or meeting place of the Belgae. Recognising its strategic importance, the Romans made it an administrative capital, and it grew to become the fifth largest city in Britain.

The River Itchen was diverted, many fine Roman town houses were built, and a street grid within the city was laid out in the typical Roman manner. William Thorn Warren in *Warren's Guide to Winchester*, first published in 1836, noted that the city's general plan was 'almost identical with what it was when the Roman cohorts were here situated'. Two centuries later, you can still see what he meant. Certainly it was the Romans who made Winchester a natural county town. Their roads radiated outwards from the city like the spokes of a wheel.

Completing the transport network was the River Itchen itself, whose presence was crucial to the way the city developed. Navigable at the time, the river connected the future Winchester with the future Southampton and therefore with continental trade. In AD 70 the fortress settlement of Clausentum was established in what is today the Southampton suburb of Bitterne. It became an important trading port, but it was also a defensive outpost of Winchester.

In the second century a defensive bank and ditch were created around the town, and at the beginning of the third century a stone wall was added. The fourth century brought a period of decline before Winchester rose again, this time as the capital of the Anglo-Saxon kingdom of Wessex – a stepping stone towards its unrivalled Norman supremacy.

Wessex

Wessex was the kingdom of the West Saxons, and its first king was probably Cerdic, reigning from 519 to 534. Replacing what is now Dorchester-on-Thames, Winchester emerged as its capital, presiding over a huge swathe of central southern and south-western England.

Wessex's importance rose in direct proportion to the damage the Vikings inflicted on its rivals Mercia, East Anglia and Northumbria, paving the way for Wessex to establish itself as the pre-eminent kingdom in Anglo-Saxon England and the spearhead for the Saxon fightback against the Danes. In effect, Wessex was the nucleus for the kingdom of England which emerged as a unified state in the tenth century.

The name Wessex fell into disuse after the Norman Conquest in the eleventh century, but was revived in the nineteenth century by the novelist Thomas

Hardy, among others. Today the name continues in the title given to Elizabeth II's youngest son, the Earl of Wessex.

WINCHESTER PLACES

Winchester's Old Minster

Winchester's Norman cathedral is the city's great landmark, but it was not the city's first great church. Winchester had earlier been home to the most important royal church of Anglo-Saxon England. Known as **Old Minster**, its outline is traced in red brick, just to the north of the present cathedral.

Cynegils, King of the West Saxons, was baptised in 635, and his son Cenwalh built the first Christian church in Winchester in about 648. The church became a cathedral when Wine (or Wini) was consecrated the first Bishop of Winchester in 660, serving a diocese which stretched from the English Channel to the river Thames. As Winchester's importance grew, so too did Old Minster, a major place of pilgrimage and a burial site for the West Saxon kings. Cnut (or Canute), his wife Emma and their son Harthacnut were buried in Old Minster; Edward the Confessor was crowned there in 1043.

Old Minster was originally a cross-shaped building, but wings were added, and so too was a memorial building, complete with tower, over St Swithun's tomb. The 990s saw further significant additions as the church became ever grander, in line with Winchester's development as a royal city.

Ealhswith, Alfred's queen, founded Nunnaminster, a nunnery, close by where there is now the Abbey Gardens; Edward the Elder, Alfred's son, founded **New Minster** next to Old Minster in 901. By the start of the eleventh century, Winchester's south-east quarter offered a remarkable collection of royal and monastic buildings.

WINCHESTER PEOPLE

Swithun, a Saintly Weather Forecaster

St Swithun's day if thou dost rain
For forty days it will remain
St Swithun's day if thou be fair
For forty days 'twill rain nae mare

Saint Swithun (or Swithin) is one of those Winchester characters who are genuinely larger than life. His earthly achievements, which were many, are completely overshadowed by his posthumous reputation as a weather forecaster. According to tradition, the weather on Swithun's feast day (15 July) will continue for forty days. It's a remarkable legacy for a man so unpromisingly named – the general consensus is that Swithun means 'pig man'.

Swithun, who died around 862, was an Anglo-Saxon Bishop of Winchester and subsequently patron saint of Winchester Cathedral. Demonstrating his humility as he lay dying, Swithun asked to be buried out of doors. He was duly buried just outside the west door of Winchester's Old Minster. There, just as he wished, people walked across his grave and the rain hammered down on his resting place.

A century later, Swithun had been made a saint, and the feeling was that he needed to be brought inside. On 15 July 971 the move was made, and his bones were reburied in a shrine inside the minster. It seems there was a heavy rainstorm either during this ceremony or on its anniversary; the storm lasted forty days and forty nights; and for many, the connection was made. The obvious conclusion was that Swithun was less than pleased at having his wishes so roundly ignored.

Even so, his transfer was associated with tales of miracles – mostly cures – happening in his name, and his reputation grew still further – so much so that in the eleventh century, Swithun was on the move again, this time into Winchester's new Norman cathedral. Swithun's reliquary was placed behind the high altar, where it attracted pilgrims in large numbers. His relics were transferred to a new site in the retrochoir in the fifteenth century, but his shrine was destroyed during the Reformation (1538).

Only one miracle relates to Swithun's lifetime. Workmen had apparently broken the eggs an old lady was carrying. One version has it that she was jostled as she crossed a bridge. Other versions suggest the incident may have been malicious. Either way, Swithun simply picked up the broken eggs, and miraculously they were whole again.

Winchester City Mill

Winchester's **Mill House** is a working watermill in the heart of the city. Powered by the River Itchen, the present mill (rebuilt in 1743), stands on the site of a medieval one. It is cared for by the National Trust, which undertook an extensive restoration project with the result that in March 2004 the mill once again started to grind corn into flour. The Trust has sensitively reinterpreted the mill's history with lively visitor displays. The City Bridge close by, dating back to 1813, is believed to stand on the site of a bridge built by St Swithun.

King Alfred the Great

*If any one man can be said to have laid
the foundations of the British Empire, that
man was Alfred the Great, King of the West
Saxons. If any place can claim to be the
nucleus around which grew up the British
Empire, that place is Winchester, capital of
Alfred's kingdom of Wessex.*
THE STORY OF WINCHESTER, W. LLOYD
WOODLAND (J. M. DENT & SONS, 1932)

He probably wouldn't have won *The Great British
Bake Off*, but **Alfred** (849–899) remains arguably
our greatest Briton – the only king in our history
to be called Great, a pre-Conquest superman who
responded in our hour of need and shaped our
entire nation.

More than a thousand years after his triumphs, his statue stands proud on the Winchester skyline – a worthy tribute to a giant among men.

King of the West Saxons, Alfred fought off the Viking invaders, established himself as the dominant ruler in the country and proceeded to rule with wisdom and mercy. A man of learning, he was a reformer, a statesman and a lawgiver. Many would argue that even if he hadn't had to fight a single battle, he would still have been our greatest monarch.

The architect of a united England, he was also the founder of our navy, a far-sighted town planner, the father of English prose, our first advocate of education for all and a noted patron of the Church.

Much of what we know of Alfred comes down to us thanks to a biography written by Bishop Asser. Revisionist historians doubt its objectivity and accuracy because it was written during Alfred's lifetime, but not even the sourest of revisionists will ever dent Alfred's standing as one of the very few genuinely towering figures in our nation's history.

But for all his great works, the story that still defines him is the story of the cakes he is alleged to have burnt in an understandably distracted moment.

Born in Wantage in present-day Oxfordshire, Alfred was already an experienced soldier by the time he came to the throne in 871, a succession which forced him to confront the persistent Viking threat. The critical moment came in 878 when the Vikings re-entered Wessex. Disaster threatened. Alfred was forced to retreat to the marshes of Athelney in Somerset, and it is here that the legend of the cakes seems to have started. A peasant woman apparently gave him shelter and, not realising just whom she was harbouring, she left him to watch over some cakes cooking in an oven. Not surprisingly, his mind was on other things, and he let them burn.

Whatever the truth, it was from Athelney that Alfred emerged to win a decisive victory over the Danes at Edington in May 878. It was a desperate last stand, but the result turned the course of our nation's history. After triumph on the battlefield, Alfred devoted himself to a monumental process of rebuilding and reinvention which touched on all aspects of the country's life. The Viking retreat left London in Alfred's possession, and Alfred had the foresight to ensure his victory would last. He fortified towns and ordered the construction of warships to defend the coast. This done, he turned his attention to the promotion of learning in his kingdom. Winchester was his capital, and Alfred made it a great centre of commerce, scholarship and religion.

Alfred died on 26 October 899, aged fifty, and was buried at Winchester. His presumed gravesite can be visited at the ruins of the city's Hyde Abbey.

WINCHESTER PEOPLE

King Cnut

*Much of the story of Winchester is the story
of the Kings of England and before then the
Kings of Wessex.*
WINCHESTER RURAL DISTRICT OFFICIAL GUIDE
(WINCHESTER INCORPORATED CHAMBER OF
COMMERCE, 1965)

Viking attacks resumed in the 980s, eventually bringing **Cnut** or **Canute** (985 or 995–1035), to the throne. Born in Denmark, Cnut became King of England in 1016, King of Denmark in 1018 and King of Norway in 1028. Effectively he ruled a huge northern European empire, but it seems he did so wisely. In England, he found favour by sending his troops back home; under his rule, trade in the kingdom flourished.

The most famous story associated with Cnut is of his humility, told by the twelfth-century chronicler, Henry of Huntingdon. Apparently tired of obsequious courtiers, Cnut set out to show that he really wasn't as all-powerful as his fawning minions liked to tell him he was. At the summit of his power, he ordered a seat to be placed for him on the seashore – the perfect position from which to prove that he really couldn't stop the incoming tide.

He told it:

> *'Thou, too, art subject to my command, as*
> *the land on which I am seated is mine; and*
> *no one has ever resisted my commands with*
> *impunity. I command you, then, not to flow*
> *over my land, nor presume to wet the feet*
> *and the robe of your lord.' The tide, however,*
> *continuing to rise as usual, dashed over his*
> *feet and legs without respect to his royal*
> *person. Then the king leaped backwards,*
> *saying: 'Let all men know how empty and*
> *worthless is the power of kings, for there*
> *is none worthy of the name, but He whom*
> *heaven, earth, and sea obey by eternal laws.'*
> THE CHRONICLE OF HENRY OF HUNTINGDON,
> BOOK VI, CANUTE'S DEATH AND CHARACTER

Cnut was buried in Old Minster in his capital city of Winchester, where he had proved himself a great benefactor. His bones are now said to lie thoroughly jumbled with those of other pre-Conquest kings in mortuary chests in the Norman cathedral which replaced Old Minster. As W. Lloyd Woodland puts it in *The Story of Winchester* (1932), 'their dry yellow bones', mingling 'in quaint juxtaposition', are 'but poor reminders of their vigorous fleshly days'. The chests are the last resting place for the mortal remains of:

Cynegils, King of Wessex (reigned 611–643)
Cenwalh, King of Wessex (643–672)
Egbert, King of Wessex (802–839)
Ethelwulf, King of Wessex (839–856)
Eadred, King of England (946–955)
Eadwig, King of England but later just of Wessex and Kent (955–959)
Cnut or Canute, King of England (1016–1035)
Harthacnut, King of England (1040–1042)
Emma of Normandy, wife of Ethelred and also Cnut
William Rufus (William II), King of England (1087–1100)

One of the mortuary chests also mentions a King Edmund.

WINCHESTER PLACES

Winchester Cathedral

*It is a very moving thing to be able to look
back eight hundred years and think of those
who have trodden these self-same floors and
looked on these massive walls. This church
has been visited by almost every prince and
many a man of note in English history.*
George Kitchin (1827–1912), Dean of
Winchester, on the Cathedral's 800th
anniversary in 1893

The longest cathedral in Europe with the exception
of St Peter's in Rome, Winchester Cathedral is a
church which befits its city. Twenty kings are buried
in a building which represents all the successive styles
of architecture from the eleventh century to the
sixteenth, spanning the Conquest to the Reformation.

Winchester already had Old Minster and New Minster, but they were not enough for the Normans. Having seized the country in 1066, William the Conqueror, the first Norman king of England, determined that Winchester should have his kind of cathedral. He appointed Walkelin, Winchester's first Norman bishop, to make it happen. Recycling Old Minster as building bricks for his new church, Walkelin began construction in 1079. It was ready for service in 1093 when huge celebrations marked its consecration. Old Minster was then demolished in 1093–1094, and the nave of the new cathedral extended across part of its site.

Inevitably, given its origins, **Winchester Cathedral** is very much in the Norman Romanesque style. As the Revd Telford-Varley notes in his *Winchester* edition of the *Beautiful Britain* series (1914), the new building was typically Norman in its symbolism and harmony, its cruciform shape, its triple repetition of recurring elements (nave, choir, transept, triforium, clerestory), its calmness, its dignity and its strength. It stands today as one of the finest examples of medieval art and architecture in existence. The nave is considered to be the best of all late Gothic naves in Europe.

Sidney Heath in his 1911 book *Winchester* captures perfectly the cathedral's special, very particular atmosphere. As he says, from the outside 'the vista of the whole block of masonry, with its stumpy tower and heavily buttressed walls, conveys the idea of immense strength rather than of gracefulness.' But when you enter the nave, you immediately appreciate the cathedral's full beauty and its vast Norman proportions:

To the receptive mind all our ancient
cathedrals, and a few of our modern ones,
possess a subtle atmosphere of their own,
indescribable but plainly felt, both within and
without their walls. In such an atmosphere

we lose sight of the Winchester of to-day. It
becomes ancient, ecclesiastical, historical,
learned, and romantic.
WINCHESTER, SIDNEY HEATH
(BLACKIE AND SON, 1911)

Despite the increasing influence of London, it was thanks to its cathedral that Winchester retained its pre-eminence as a centre of learning and religion throughout the medieval period.

At the entrance to the cathedral grounds stands one of Winchester's most striking pieces of modern art, *Luminous Motion* by Peter Freeman. Installed in 2002, it offers an interactive light column. Send it a text, and fibre optic lights change colour accordingly in its tall column of stainless steel.

Winchester Castle
and Great Hall

*Outwardly Winchester retains today little
impress of the great Saxon period which
first made her so prominent. The Norman
Conquest was not an occupation merely,
it was a deluge.*

BEAUTIFUL BRITAIN: WINCHESTER, REVD
TELFORD-VARLEY (ADAM & CHARLES BLACK, 1914)

It is difficult to overestimate the impact the
Normans had on Winchester; they swept aside so
much of what had gone before. The Normans gave
Winchester its cathedral; they also gave it its castle,
of which now only the Great Hall remains, one of the
finest surviving aisled halls of the thirteenth century.
Determined to secure his hold on the city after his
Conquest of 1066, William I ordered the construction

of **Winchester Castle** in 1067; it became one of the most important buildings in the country, home to crucial elements of government including the Treasury and the Exchequer. The Great Hall, which can be visited today, was where the first Parliaments of England were held. The castle itself occupied this and adjoining land to the south-west.

View the castle as part of the rich tapestry of Norman Winchester, and you start to glimpse the remarkable city Winchester presented in the eleventh and twelfth centuries – a city with a magnificent cathedral, important monasteries and more than fifty parish churches, all within its high strong walls. Home also to one of the country's great trading fairs, the city expanded dramatically, rivalling Norwich as second in size only to London.

Winchester's influence diminished after the twelfth century as government transferred to London, but the castle remained a place of great royal significance for the next five centuries. Here Henry III was born in 1207; here Arthur, eldest son of Henry VII, was born in 1486; and here Henry VIII entertained the Emperor Charles V in 1522. It was also here that Mary I and Philip II of Spain celebrated their wedding in 1554.

By the thirteenth century, the castle was in need of repair and restoration. The Great Hall was built between 1222 and 1235 under Henry III, and his son Edward I continued his good work, though in 1302, Edward and his wife Margaret of France were lucky to escape with their lives when the royal apartments were destroyed by fire. Three and a half centuries later, after the Parliamentary forces captured the castle from the defending Royalists in 1646, Oliver Cromwell ordered the castle's demolition. Just the Great Hall remained, kept as a venue for assemblies and the county assizes, a function which later provided a grim chapter in the building's history.

As part of the Bloody Assizes in 1685, Judge Jeffreys passed sentence of death in the Great Hall on the supporters of the Duke of Monmouth. Earlier, Sir Walter Raleigh had also received sentence of death in this very room in 1603.

The Great Hall retained its legal function into the twentieth century. The *Winchester Rural District Official Guide*, 1965, notes that it is 'at present a temporary court for Assizes and Quarter sessions pending construction of four new courts to the east of Castle Hall'. The new Crown Courts were built between 1965 and 1974 and opened by the Lord Chancellor, Lord Hailsham.

These days, the Great Hall's principal feature is its Round Table on the wall. Close to the Great Hall is the only other remnant of the castle – the ruins of a tower from its walls. Restored passageways in the basement of the tower lead out to the dry moat which would have surrounded the castle.

Just outside Winchester's Great Hall is **Queen Eleanor's Garden**, a recreation by Sylvia Landsberg of an enclosed medieval garden, with plants that would have been grown in the thirteenth century, among them holly, ivy, bay, roses, columbine and strawberry plants. It is named after two Queen Eleanors: Queen Eleanor of Provence and her daughter-in-law, Queen Eleanor of Castile, who would have enjoyed just such a garden. It was opened by Queen Elizabeth, the Queen Mother, as part of the Domesday 900 celebrations in 1986.

Domesday Book

When you've conquered a land, there comes a moment when you simply have to sit back and take stock. That moment came for William I with the **Domesday Book**, a monumental undertaking in which he sent men to every shire to find out how much each landholder had in land and livestock and what it was worth. The great survey, which covered much of England and parts of Wales, was completed in 1086, with the results collated in the Domesday Book, which is now held in the National Archives at Kew. Given Winchester's importance in those early Norman years, it comes as no surprise that Winchester was central to the vast operation. The returns from each county were gathered in Winchester.

Some parts of the survey were later lost; and Winchester and London were among the places not included. Some historians say the surveys from such places were not transcribed; others that the towns were omitted because of their complexity.

However, Winchester did catch up, with the **Survey of Winchester** (*c*.1103–1115), a glimpse into a city which boasted some wonderful sounding street names including Snithelingastret, Bredenestret, Scowertenestret, Alwarenestret, Flescmangerstret, Wongarstret, Tannerstret and Bucchestret.

WINCHESTER PLACES

God Begot House

Winchester's **God Begot House** stands on the High Street, on the the site of the ancient manor of God Begot which Emma, widow of King Cnut, bequeathed to St Swithun's Priory in 1052. God Begot probably means something like 'the goods getter' or 'a good bargain'.

The manor made its own laws, effectively existing outside normal jurisdictions. As such, it became a refuge for anyone on the run. Contemporary records make it clear than any man or woman accused of any felony could claim the liberty of God Begot and therefore dwell safely inside. Only ministers of the priory and convent of St Swithun held sway within its confines. Officers of the king had no authority to enter.

And so it continued until the dissolution of the monasteries under Henry VIII when its rights and privileges were taken away. The present building, God Begot House, is built of brick and half-timber work and dates from the middle of the sixteenth century. It is currently an Italian restaurant.

Some Great Bishops of Winchester

The Rt Revd Tim Dakin was enthroned on 21 April 2012 as the ninety-seventh Bishop of Winchester, joining an illustrious line stretching back to the seventh century. Many of his predecessors have been bishops of distinction.

[Bishop Henry de Blois was a] masterful man and a scheming politician, but high-minded withal, and intensely loyal to Holy Church

BEAUTIFUL BRITAIN: WINCHESTER, REVD
TELFORD-VARLEY (ADAM & CHARLES BLACK, 1914)

Grandchild of William the Conqueror, **Henry de Blois** (1098/9–1171) was one of Winchester's greatest bishops, a skilled mediator who negotiated dangerously choppy political waters while managing to serve his Church. He was a diplomat in a difficult century; a man of huge personal wealth who prized independence of mind, particularly his own.

Henry de Blois was brought to England by Henry I, becoming Abbot of Glastonbury in 1126 and Bishop of Winchester three years later. He retained both offices for forty years. Henry played an important part in helping his older brother Stephen become king, but relations with his brother deteriorated when Henry was passed over for the archbishopric of Canterbury. In the civil war known as The Anarchy (1135–1153), in which Stephen was captured at the battle of Lincoln on 2 February 1141, Henry initially sided with the Empress Matilda against him before switching his support back to his brother. When the empress rode into Winchester, Henry helped rally King Stephen's forces and was instrumental in forcing her retreat. Later that year, Stephen was restored to power.

Henry was buried in Winchester Cathedral, but it is not known precisely where. It is now generally believed that he is the occupant of the tomb in the chancel previously believed to contain the remains of William Rufus.

Two of his great legacies in Winchester are the Hospital of St Cross (which he founded between 1132 and 1136), and the Palace of Wolvesey (which he began in 1138). He was also a great collector, leaving Winchester a rich treasure of relics and gold and silver work on his death. Henry's other important legacy is the magnificent Winchester Bible which it is believed he commissioned in 1160.

*Interesting and important as are the
association of Alfred and St Swithun with
this ancient capital of Wessex, the genius
loci is William of Wykeham, one of the most
remarkable men the world has ever produced.
The more we study his life and character the
more we are amazed at the versatile nature of
his splendid gifts.*

WINCHESTER, SIDNEY HEATH
(BLACKIE AND SON, 1911)

William of Wykeham's achievements are quite extraordinary. Born to a peasant family in Wickham, 15 miles south of Winchester, William (1320 or 1324 –1404) rose to become Bishop of Winchester and Chancellor of England. Along the way, he founded New College, Oxford (1379) and Winchester College (1382), the oldest continuously running school in the country. He also built a large part of Windsor Castle.

Both Winchester College and New College adopted his motto 'Manners Makyth Man', and were models for later colleges including Eton and King's College, Cambridge. In Winchester, his contribution to the cathedral was to remodel the nave in the Perpendicular style.

Stephen Gardiner (*c.*1495–1555) was Bishop of Winchester from 1531 to 1551 and again from 1553 to 1555. The author of *De vera obedientia* (*On True Obedience,* 1535) in Henry VIII's support, Gardiner helped secure Henry's divorce from Catherine of Aragon. At his peak, he was one of the most influential courtier-prelates of his day, serving as one of Henry's key ministers from 1542 until Henry's death in 1547.

Gardiner was imprisoned in the Tower of London from 1548 to 1551 under Edward VI and deprived of his see, but his star rose again with Mary I who restored him to Winchester and made him Lord Chancellor in August 1553. Posthumously he fell victim to the English Civil War when his carved memorial skeleton in the Cathedral was attacked by Parliamentarian troops.

Successively Bishop of Chichester (1605), Ely (1609) and Winchester (1618), **Lancelot Andrewes** (1555–1626) became Dean of Westminster in 1601. He was prominent at the courts of Elizabeth I and James I and gave us Guy Fawkes Night, or Bonfire Night as it is more commonly called these days. Following the discovery of the failed Gunpowder Plot of 1605, Andrewes argued that the nation's and the Church of England's deliverance by God should be celebrated annually – a custom still observed every year on 5 November.

T. S. Eliot observed that Andrewes' sermons rank with the finest English prose of their time: 'He takes a word and derives a world from it; squeezing and squeezing the word until it yields a full juice of meaning which we never should have supposed any word to possess.'

WINCHESTER PLACES

Wolvesey Castle and the Bishop's House

Winchester can claim a distinction as one of the few cities in the country with two castles: the king's on the hillside, of which only the Great Hall remains, and the bishop's at Wolvesey. Today **Wolvesey Castle** stands as extensive ruins which can do no more than hint at the time when it was one of the most impressive buildings in the country.

Wolvesey Castle was part of Henry de Blois' grand plan to turn Winchester into an archbishopric to rival Canterbury, and he began building his fortified palace in 1138. After a 1302 fire in the royal apartments at the king's castle, Wolvesey Castle instead became Winchester's royal accommodation of choice. It was here that Mary I and Philip II of Spain held their wedding breakfast on 25 July 1554.

Sadly, the fate of Wolvesey Castle was to mirror that of Winchester Castle when it was destroyed by the Parliamentarian forces during the English Civil War.

A new episcopal palace was built on the site, close to the castle ruins, for Bishop Morley in 1684, but it wasn't used consistently and fell into disrepair. Under Bishop Brownlow North in 1786, the eastern and main south wings were demolished. The remaining wing was eventually restored in the 1920s, since when it has once again been the **Bishop's House**, home to the bishops of Winchester.

WINCHESTER TIMES

'And every one was an 'Enery'

Henry I (1068–1135) was the fourth and youngest son of William I, and for a while the view – largely dismissed now – was that he murdered his way to the throne, getting rid of his older brother William Rufus and then dashing to Winchester to claim the kingdom. It seems more likely that the arrow which killed William was fired accidentally, but the dash to Winchester certainly happened. Henry had to act fast to prevent his oldest brother Robert Curthose, Duke of Normandy, succeeding to the throne. Once at Winchester, the future Henry I seized control of the Treasury, won the support of a rump group of barons and then set off to Westminster to be crowned.

As king, Henry's fine administrative skills brought him the nickname Beauclerc. It seems likely that he originated the Exchequer, which met at Winchester and marked an important step towards modern government. In another inspired moment, he brought across to England Henry de Blois, who was to prove one of the greatest and most influential bishops of Winchester. Henry I reigned from 1100 to 1135.

At the heart of the civil war known as The Anarchy (1135–1153) was a dispute between Empress Matilda and her cousin King Stephen of England over the English crown. It was ended by the Treaty of Winchester of 1153, whereby it was agreed that Stephen would keep the throne until his death but was obliged to recognise as his heir Matilda's son Henry of Anjou, the future **Henry II,** the first Plantangenet king. Stephen and Henry met at Winchester to work out the terms of the treaty which was witnessed at Westminster. Henry reigned from 1154 to 1189.

Henry III (1207–1272), King of England from 1216 to 1272, liked to call himself Henry of Winchester in honour of his birthplace. He was born in Winchester Castle and baptised in the cathedral. While still a young man, he modernised the castle and built the Great Hall, the only part of the Castle which still stands today and the place where Henry III held Parliament.

Henry IV (1366–1413), known as Henry Bolingbroke, was King of England from 1399 to 1413. Henry IV and his second wife Joan of Navarre (1368–1437) were married in Winchester Cathedral on 7 February 1403. She remained in England after Henry's death and was buried beside him in Canterbury Cathedral. One of the most important men in England under Henry IV was his half-brother Henry Beaufort, Bishop of Winchester (served 1404–1447) and three times Chancellor of England, the first time from 1403 to 1405.

Henry V (1386–1422) was King of England from 1413 to 1422, and once again Henry Beaufort, Bishop of Winchester, was an important figure during his reign. Beaufort had fallen foul of Henry IV when he had sided with the future Henry V against him. When Henry V became king, he repaid Beaufort's support by making him Chancellor for a second time (1413–1417). While Henry V fought in France, Beaufort, his uncle, effectively ruled supreme.

Henry VI (1421–1471), son of Henry V, was King of England from 1422 to 1461, acceding to the throne at the age of just nine months. Inevitably, Bishop Henry Beaufort, his great-uncle, had an important part to play in his early life. The nobles swore loyalty to the baby king, and a regency council was appointed to run the country until he came of age. Henry Beaufort was a key member. His third stint as Chancellor of England, under his third Henry, was from 1424 to 1426.

Henry VII (1457–1509) was the first Tudor king. He was also the last king of England to win his throne on the field of battle, when he defeated Richard III at the Battle of Bosworth Field. He reigned from 1485 to 1509, and it was certainly to strengthen his position that he chose for his firstborn, Arthur, to be born in the country's ancient capital, Winchester, a place wrapped up in the legends of King Arthur – legends which held a strong fascination for Henry. Prince Arthur was born in Winchester in September 1486 and was christened in the cathedral amid rich medieval pageantry. Tragically, his life was to be a short one, and he died at the age of 15 on 2 April 1502. Henry VII was succeeded instead by his younger son, Henry VIII.

Henry VIII (1491–1547) was King of England from 1509 until his death. It is widely accepted that the face on Winchester's celebrated Round Table is his; like his father Henry VII before him, he wanted a little bit of the great Arthurian legend. Henry VIII entertained the Holy Roman Emperor Charles V in Winchester in 1522, continuing the city's proud tradition of royal occasions and ceremony, but otherwise Henry VIII's principal impact on Winchester came with the dissolution of the city's three monastic institutions and the destruction of St Swithun's shrine in the Cathedral. Seven years after Henry VIII's death, his older daughter Mary was married in Winchester Cathedral.

Hyde Abbey

History has done few favours to Winchester's **Hyde Abbey**, of which only the gatehouse remains today, a rectangular stone building dating back to the fifteenth century. The Abbey's construction was ordered by Henry I and the result was one of the most impressive Romanesque buildings in the country, consecrated with due ceremony in 1110. The monks walked in procession there with their relics and also with the bodies of Alfred, his wife Ealhswith and his son Edward the Elder, all previously buried in New Minster.

Interpretative panels at the site today give a clear idea of the huge scale of the former abbey which was made up of three main areas – the forecourt, the inner courtyard and the main monastic courtyard – all enclosed within the precinct walls.

The building was damaged during the Rout of Winchester (1141) along with much of the city; worse, however, was to come in 1538 during the dissolution of the monasteries under Henry VIII. The treasure was plundered, and the buildings were demolished and turned into materials for other constructions elsewhere – all except for the gatehouse.

The Friends of Hyde Abbey Garden was set up following a community archaeology excavation in 1999, and the Friends have now recreated the outline of the eastern end of the abbey's church. They have also marked the likely site of the graves of Alfred and his family. The garden was opened on 2 June 2003, on the fiftieth anniversary of the coronation of Elizabeth II. You can view the three gravestones through a glass panel which eerily resurrects the Abbey church around them.

Warring Matildas and the Rout of Winchester

Henry I determined that his daughter, the Empress Matilda, should succeed him; but when he died, it was his nephew, Stephen de Blois, who seized power, helped by his brother, Henry de Blois, Bishop of Winchester. The result was The Anarchy, a civil war which lasted from 1135 to 1153.

Matilda arrived in England from France in 1139 to lead her supporters, but initially neither side gained an advantage. With the help of her half-brother, Robert of Gloucester, Matilda took the south-west while Stephen largely retained the south-east.

However, a turning point came in 1141 when Stephen was captured and effectively deposed at the Battle of Lincoln. Matilda tried to claim the crown in London, but she was forced back

Empress Matilda

by hostile crowds. And then came the **Rout of Winchester** – an event in which Bishop Henry played a crucial role.

Stephen's treatment of other bishops had opened up a rift between Church and state; Henry seems generally to have been motivated by the desire for peace and a desire to retain and increase his own standing. Having first sided with his brother, Bishop Henry swapped sides in support of Matilda, welcoming her to Winchester and seeing her installed in the royal castle.

However, another Matilda now played her part in the proceedings. Queen Matilda, wife of the imprisoned Stephen, was among those who now persuaded Henry to switch his allegiance back to her husband.

Henry therefore set about regaining Winchester for the king's cause. His men now besieged the Empress Matilda's forces in Winchester Castle. Matilda's response was a strong one, sending her own forces in turn, obliging Henry to retreat into his fortified episcopal palace, Wolvesey Castle. When Queen Matilda rode to the rescue, the two Matildas went to war in a curious double blockade. Queen Matilda besieged the city inside which Empress Matilda besieged Bishop Henry's men in his castle.

Inevitably, it was the city that suffered. Fire broke out, most likely started by the bishop's men, and Wolvesey, St Mary's Nunnaminster, Hyde Abbey and the Royal Palace were all damaged. After a month, the Empress Matilda was forced to make a break for it. Robert brought up the rearguard to protect her as she departed, but Queen Matilda attacked the moment they left. The Empress Matilda got away, but Robert was captured. Both sides swapped their captives, a deal which allowed Stephen to resume his kingship and lost the Empress the advantage she had gained at Lincoln. Stephen was back in business and promptly besieged the Empress at Oxford. The war rolled on for years to come until the **Treaty of Winchester** (1153) brought a negotiated peace.

Winchester was left with a legacy of loss and ruin amid the flames and the pillaging. The Queen's London militia sacked the city. Houses, shops and churches were all reduced to rubble; people were tortured and executed. It was not until the time of William of Wykeham (1320 or 1324–1404) that the city's fortunes revived.

WINCHESTER PLACES

Gates to the City

Westgate and **Kingsgate** are the only two surviving fortified gateways in Winchester. Northgate, Southgate and Eastgate were all demolished in 1791, in too poor a condition to warrant restoration. For centuries, all the gates would have been locked at night as part of the city's defences.

Standing on the site of an earlier Roman gate, the Westgate is mostly thirteenth century. On the north side you can still see where the gate joined the surrounding city wall. Given its narrowness, it is remarkable that the Westgate was in use until 1959 when the High Street was finally routed around it. A

pedestrian walkway through the gate was added in 1791, knocking through the porter's lodge.

It seems likely that the Westgate escaped the fate of the other gates in the city because it was used as a smoking room for the adjacent hotel. It was acquired by the City Corporation in the nineteenth century, becoming a museum in 1898 and also home to the city archives. It continues as a museum today, following extensive renovation. Visitors can still see the graffiti on the walls from its 150 years as a debtors' prison. They can also enjoy the Westgate Museum's collection of weights and measures and a Tudor ceiling from Winchester College.

The Kingsgate is probably fourteenth century, with the pedestrian walkways added in the eighteenth century. The name Kingsgate at this site was first recorded in 1148. Above it is the exquisite church of St Swithun-upon-Kingsgate, one of Winchester's great gems. Built in the Early English style, it counts among its rare distinctions the fact that it is effectively part of the old city walls. Approached up steep steps, it impresses with its simplicity. Rectangular in shape, the church has no division between nave and chancel. The way the light falls through its windows is a photographer's dream. The parish registers date back to 1562 for baptisms and burials, and to 1564 for marriages.

Close to the Westgate is the life-size bronze *Horse and Rider*, a sculpture by noted British sculptor and printmaker Dame Elisabeth Frink (1930–1993). Nearby, just outside County Hall is David Kemp's bronze *Hampshire Hog*, installed to mark the centenary of Hampshire County Council in 1989. The Hampshire (black with a white belt) is a noted domestic pig breed especially popular in the USA, but since the late eighteenth century, 'Hampshire hog' has also been a nickname for Hampshire residents.

Also near the Westgate is an obelisk erected in 1759 to mark an outbreak of the plague in Winchester in 1669. Farmers would bring their produce to the city and leave it outside the gate for the city's plague-stricken inhabitants, who would leave their payment in bowls of vinegar in the hope of preventing the disease from spreading. The country-dwellers would use pincers to pick out the coins. The transactions took place on the stone which forms the base of the obelisk.

Scandal in the City

Emma of Normandy's seemingly impeccable lineage was not enough to convince the world of her innocence. Despite being wife to two kings, Ethelred and Canute, and mother to two others, Harthacnut and Edward the Confessor, Emma (*c.* 985–1052) had to walk on red-hot ploughshares to prove that she really hadn't been having her wicked way with Aelfwine, Bishop of Winchester from 1032 to 1047. She was charged with criminal familiarity and insisted on undergoing trial by ordeal which she duly accomplished in the city's minster, emerging unhurt – confirmation that not only was she irreproachable, but, more importantly for her, so too was the bishop. Seemingly, it helped that she spent the night before praying at the shrine of St Swithun, who appeared before her and obligingly tipped her the wink: 'I am St Swithun whom you have invoked; fear not, the fire shall do you no hurt.'

The country's first brothels sprang up in Southwark where Roman soldiers guarded the Thames crossing. In medieval times, London's Bankside brothels were part of the vast diocese of Winchester. They were regulated by Henry II in the twelfth century and **Winchester geese** became the nickname for the South Bank prostitutes in the 'stews' (brothels) that were licensed by the Bishop of Winchester in the area around his London palace. The Church took the view that the income was useful to both bishop and king alike. Controls became much tighter when syphilis first spread in the early sixteenth century. By extension, to be 'bitten by a Winchester goose' meant to catch syphilis.

Henry Garnett (1555–1606) was a Jesuit executed for his complicity in the Gunpowder Plot of 1605. Depending on which account you trust, he may or may not also have been a naughty boy at Winchester College where he was elected a scholar in 1567.

One account asserts that he was 'the prime scholar of Winchester College, very skilful in music and in playing upon the instruments, very modest in his countenance and in all his actions, so much that the schoolmasters and wardens offered him very great friendship'; alternatively, 'Garnet was guilty at Winchester not only of the grossest immorality, but of a precocious display of his aptitude for plots, probably unique in schoolboy annals.' The suggestion is that he plotted to cut off the right hand of the headmaster – though the chances are that such tales are a little bit of retrospective blackening by his enemies.

Little is known of **Judith Phillips**, *alias* Doll, save to say that she was a confidence trickster who preyed on the unwary in the south of England in the late sixteenth century and that she was once sentenced to death in Salisbury for her deceits, only to be pardoned. The pamphlet *The Brideling, Sadling and Ryding, of a Rich Churle in Hampshire* (1595) chronicles her most spectacular crime in which she duped a Hampshire farmer and his wife in the village of Upsborne. Burying some coins which she then pretended to find, she soon had the farmer in her power. To cut a long story short, the farmer ended up on all fours with a saddle on his back. Doll rode him around the garden, then told him to shut his eyes and made off with his money. Realising how daft he had been, the farmer then hastened to Winchester where he raised a hue and cry. Doll was there brought before the assizes, confessed and was punished – but was soon back to her old ways.

William Franklin or **Frankelin** (*b. c.*1610) was apparently Christ reincarnated – or so he liked to tell the world. A rope-maker from London, he was 'somewhat distracted in his brain' by the plague and was bled several times to relieve his sufferings. During the bleedings, he was alleged to have said he was God and Christ. Franklin repented but then went further, claiming to have 'received some Revelations and Visions' and that he had the gift of prophecy. He persuaded a certain **Mary Gadbury** (*b. c.*1619) that he was the Son of God come to earth in 'a new body', and together they set off for a new life together in Hampshire, where after various adventures, Franklin started to attract followers to his belief that he was 'ye Christ crucified without ye gates of Jerusalem, ye son of god & saviour of ye world'. Franklin and three of his supporters were arrested and taken to Winchester in 1650 where he agreed to recant.

Winchester-born physician and theological writer **William Coward** had the unhappy distinction of having his books effectively put to death. Born around 1656, he published *Second Thoughts Concerning Human Soul* (1702), under the rather unconvincing pseudonym Estibius Psychalethes, and was accused of atheism. The House of Commons condemned his writings and ordered his books to be burnt by the common hangman.

When Charles II visited Winchester to oversee the construction of his planned new palace, he asked Thomas Ken (1637–1711), one of the king's chaplains and a Prebend of Winchester Cathedral, to accommodate his mistress Nell Gwyn (1650–1687)

in his prebendal house. Ken refused, and Nell had to stay in the deanery. Fortunately for Ken, Charles respected him for his principled stance, though he was alleged to have later referred to him as 'the ugly little man who wouldn't give poor Nelly lodging'. Other variations exist. Charles is also reported to have said, 'I must go and hear little Ken tell me of my faults.' However, when a vacancy arose for a new bishop at Bath and Wells, Charles was apparently determined that the position should be Ken's. 'Where is the good little man that refused his lodging to poor Nell?' he asked admiringly – or so the story goes.

Astrologer **Thomas White** died in 1813 after three months in prison in Winchester. He had been arrested and charged under the Vagrancy Act for 'pretending and professing to tell Fortunes'. At the time of his arrest, White was living on the Isle of Wight. He was approached by a police informer who then paid him with marked money. White was the author of *The Beauties of Occult Science Investigated, or, The Celestial Intelligencer* (1810).

Here's an alumnus Winchester College is probably not keen to recall: **Sir Oswald Mosley** (1896–1980), the notorious British fascist leader. After Winchester, he trained at the Royal Military College, Sandhurst, served in World War One and entered Parliament for Harrow in 1918. Variously a Conservative, an Independent and a Labour Party supporter, he set up the New Party and then, following a visit to Italy in 1932, he created the British Union of Fascists which became increasingly anti-Semitic as the 1930s progressed.

'It's not cricket' is the well-known indignant response to unfair play. The Australians boomed it loud and clear when former Winchester College schoolboy **Douglas Jardine** (1900–1958) unleashed on them his fast leg theory bowling in cricket's infamous Bodyline series, the 1932–1933 Ashes tour of Australia. As captain of Winchester College cricket team, Jardine scored 997 runs at an average of 66.46, on top of which he was applauded for his tactical shrewdness – something he showed once again when he believed he had found a way to negate the almost other-worldly brilliance of the great Aussie batsman, Sir Donald Bradman. The idea was to bowl the ball so short on the line of the leg stump that it rose sharply towards the batsman's body. The cricketing world cried foul, and the laws of cricket were changed to prevent a repetition.

Organist, harpsichordist and conductor **Martin Neary** was born in London in 1940 and served as organist at Winchester Cathedral from 1972 to 1988.

He was then appointed organist at Westminster Abbey (1988–1998) where he was the musical director of the funeral service for Diana, Princess of Wales. However, less than a year later, he was sacked on the grounds of gross misconduct. Dr Neary petitioned the Queen, as Visitor of the Abbey, to resolve the dispute, but the dismissal was upheld. The nub of the matter was a company that Neary and his wife had set up, without the Dean's knowledge, to handle the business side of the Abbey's musical life. Lord Jauncey, who determined the matter, found that the Nearys had not been dishonest, but nonetheless supported the Dean's decision to sack him.

The Hospital of St Cross

Around three-quarters of a mile to the south of Winchester lies the **Hospital of St Cross**, the finest, largest and oldest medieval almshouse in the country. It was founded between 1132 and 1136 by William the Conqueror's grandson, Bishop Henry de Blois, to accommodate 13 poor Brothers of St Cross and to feed 100 more at the gates each day. The story goes that Henry was stopped by a peasant girl who begged him to help her and her family who were reduced to starvation by the civil war which was then raging.

The establishment was extended by Cardinal Beaufort, Bishop of Winchester from 1404 to 1447, with the addition of an 'Almshouse of Noble Poverty' in 1446. Its work continues to this day as home to twenty-five elderly men, members either of the Foundation of the Hospital of St Cross or the Order of Noble Poverty, known as the Black Brothers and the Red Brothers respectively. The Hospital's church is regarded as a fine example of transitional Norman work. Visitors can still receive the Wayfarer's Dole, a small beaker of beer and a morsel of bread.

A Song in Praise of Winchester

Me lykyth ever the lenger the bet
by Wynchestyr, that joly cyte.
The toun ys good and wel yset,
the folk ys cumly on to see.
The ayr ys good, bothe yn and out.
The cyte stont bineth an hylle,
the ryvers rennyth al about.
The toun ys rulyd uppe skylle.

The song emanated from Winchester College in around 1395. The gist is that the singer likes Winchester more and more, considering it a jolly city, a good town in a good position, peopled by comely folks who have good air to breathe, both indoors and outside. The city stands on a hill with rivers running all about, with the whole town ruled with skill.

WINCHESTER PLACES

St Catherine's Hill and St Giles' Hill

Two hills have played their part in Winchester history: St Catherine's Hill, just to the south-east of the city; and St Giles' Hill to the east.

A large early Iron Age earthwork encircles **St Catherine's Hill**, dating back to about three centuries BC. It was destroyed in about 50 BC by Belgic refugees from northern Gaul who then settled on the site of the present city. Later a medieval chapel was erected on top of the hill in honour of St Catherine; a larger chapel was suppressed by Cardinal Wolsey in 1528; beech trees were planted on the summit by militia men in 1762. But for many, the hill's most interesting feature is the Mizmaze, which legend says was cut out by a bored Winchester College schoolboy who had been left behind during the summer holidays. It seems likely that the maze is medieval in origin.

Nearby is **St Giles' Hill**, which offers a splendid view directly down onto the city centre below, with the statue of Alfred in the foreground. Six centuries ago there were times when the hill would have been even busier than the city itself, for this was where the great St Giles' fair was held every September. All trading in Winchester and for some ten miles around was suspended for its duration. The fair dated back to Norman times, attracted merchants from across Europe and was progressively extended. Its normal duration was sixteen days, but it was frequently lengthened to twenty or twenty-four by temporary grants. By the time of Henry II, it was probably the finest fair in England.

WINCHESTER PEOPLE

Men of God

An important ecclesiastical centre for many centuries, Winchester has been associated with a long line of distinguished men of God.

Devon-born theologian **Theophilus Gale** (1628–1679) was appointed preacher in Winchester Cathedral in 1657. Among his writings was *Theophilie, or, A Discourse of the Saints Amitie with God in Christ* (1671). Generally regarded as his greatest work was *The Court of the Gentiles*, published in four volumes between 1669 and 1678.

Church of England clergyman **Thomas Newlin** (*d.* 1744) was the son of William Newlin, rector of St Swithun's in Winchester, where he was baptised in 1688. Educated at Winchester College, he went on to become a fellow of Magdalen College, Oxford, where he staunchly promoted education in original ancient languages, often preaching in Latin. His *One and Twenty Sermons on Several Occasions* was published in 1726.

George Frederick Nott (1767–1841), a prebendary of Winchester, was a clergyman and literary editor. As part of his duties, he oversaw the cathedral repairs, but suffered a bad fall in early 1817 from which he never fully recovered. Nott convalesced in Italy where he translated the *Book of Common Prayer* into Italian (1831). However, his reputation rests principally on his *Works of Henry Howard, Earl of Surrey, and of Sir Thomas Wyatt, the Elder* (1815–1816). Nott died in Winchester and was buried in the north transept of the cathedral.

Wiltshire-born Wesleyan Methodist **James Crabb** (1774–1851) proved himself a friend to the country's Gypsies. An itinerant preacher, he travelled extensively in the south, intent on improving the lot of the people he came across, particularly in Southampton. Crabb was drawn to society's outcasts after witnessing the harsh treatment meted out at the Winchester assizes in 1827 where a Gypsy was condemned to death for horse-stealing while his non-Gypsy accomplice was recommended for mercy. His writings included *The Gipsies' Advocate; or Observations on the origin, character, manners, and habits of the English Gipsies* (1831).

Churches and Bell Towers

The tower of the church of **St Lawrence** is so hemmed in by shops and surrounding buildings that, like the church itself, it is easy to miss, tucked away off one of Winchester's busiest shortcuts between the High Street and the cathedral. It wouldn't have been so in the days of public executions. It was the bells of St Lawrence's church which sounded the death knell for the condemned. These days, the church can rejoice in a rather happier distinction. On the way to their enthronement in Winchester Cathedral, the bishops designate of the diocese enter this ancient church to robe and 'ring themselves in'. Historians are generally agreed that the church occupies the site of the chapel royal of William the Conqueror's castle palace. Today's church is mostly fifteenth century, with a number of reused twelfth-century stones. Extensive repairs and restoration followed a fire in 1978.

Close to the ruins of Hyde Abbey is the church of **St Bartholomew**, built of flint with limestone dressings. The church is twelfth century in origin, but now surprisingly modern. The chancel was rebuilt in 1857–1859 by John Colson; the north chapel, the north transept and the aisle are all additions. The south wall of the nave and the west tower are the only old parts of the church; the tower is probably fifteenth century.

The oldest parish church in Winchester, **St John the Baptist**, also known as St John in the Soke, is partly twelfth century, but offers a fascinating trip through history as you enter its doors. Norman stonework, Tudor woodwork and Victorian stained glass are among the attractions, as are fragments of a series of wall paintings dating back to about 1280. The church is attractively situated on the slope of the hill on the east of the city. It was used by the scholars of Winchester College before the College Chapel was finished in 1395.

St John's Chapel, a rectangular building of late thirteenth-century date which still stands in The Broadway, was attached to a hospital or hospice at St John's House, a place of refuge for the old and infirm, for needy travellers passing through and for Winchester's poor. St John's Winchester Charity is one of the oldest charitable institutions in the country. It seems likely that it was founded by St Brinstan, Bishop of Winchester from 931 to 934. The charity went under the name St John's Hospital, which later became St John's Hospital and the Allied Charities. In 1984 it changed its name again, to become St John's Winchester Charity. Today the charity offers sheltered almshouse accommodation in a number of buildings in the city for older people in need.

The former **St Thomas' Church** on Southgate Street, dating from the 1840s–1850s, was mentioned in Thomas Hardy's novel *Tess of the D'Urbervilles* but today stands as a rather sorry, neglected sight.

Deconsecrated, it was converted to office and storage accommodation in the 1970s. The building became the St Thomas Centre, home to organisations including the Hampshire Association of Parish and Town Councils and the Hampshire Sculpture Trust, but today stands empty. In 2012, owners Hampshire County Council sought expressions of interest for what they called 'a unique freehold opportunity in Winchester city centre'.

The Statute of Winchester

Winchester played a crucial early role in the history of policing with the **Statute of Winchester** (1285) which effectively regularised the maintenance of law and order under Edward I. The legislation introduced justices of the peace, constables and nightwatchmen. It provided the basis for law enforcement for the next 500 years.

One significant element of the statute was its declaration that each district or 'hundred' would be held responsible for unsolved crimes. The statute was also important for the way it regularised the medieval practice of hue and cry: calling out loudly for help if you were pursuing a suspected criminal. If a crime has been witnessed, then bystanders must help apprehend the criminal – an obligation which continues to this day. It also stipulated 'At what Times the Gates of great Towns shall be shut, and when the Night Watch shall begin and end' and the 'Breadth of Highways leading from one Market-Town to another'.

Imprisoned for their Beliefs

Quaker preacher **Humphry Smith** (*bap.* 1624, *d.* 1663) was a reluctant guest in Winchester where he was imprisoned twice for his beliefs and activities. Reportedly he was a very compelling preacher. Sadly for him, however, his preaching was not always welcomed. Smith was imprisoned first in Exeter and then twice in Winchester, where he died of jail fever in 1663.

Franciscan friar **Matthew Atkinson** (1656–1729), buried in Winchester, was perhaps the last man in England to suffer perpetual life imprisonment for exercising the function of a Catholic priest. At first he was committed to Newgate prison and then held at Hurst Castle on the western approaches to the Solent, opposite the Isle of Wight. Following his death after nearly 30 years of confinement, his body was brought to Winchester by Catholic nobles.

The poet **Basil Bunting** (1900–1985) was brought up a Quaker with strong pacifist beliefs. He strongly opposed World War One and was arrested as a conscientious objector in 1918. Bunting served more than a year in Wormwood Scrubs and Winchester prison. He went on to become an important voice in British modernist poetry, best remembered for his autobiographical poem *Briggflatts*, published in 1966.

Poet **Norman Alexander MacCaig** (1910–1996) also saw the wrong side of Winchester when he was imprisoned in the city as a conscientious objector during World War Two after being called up in 1941.

When he refused to service tanks, he was court-martialled and jailed. His first collection of poetry *Far Cry* was published in 1943.

Pentonville Prison, which was built as a model prison in 1840–1842, takes its name from **Henry Penton**, MP for Winchester, who owned the site which he began developing for building in about 1773.

The Incredible Shrinking Diocese

At first, the **diocese of Winchester** stretched from the south coast to the Thames. The centuries since have seen it sharply reduced in size. Winchester is the fifth senior see after Canterbury, York, London and Durham, and, like them, its bishop always has a seat in the House of Lords. But the diocese of Winchester is just a fraction of what it used to be.

Wine was the first bishop in about 660; half a century later, the diocese was split. Hampshire, Surrey, Sussex and the Isle of Wight stayed under Winchester, but everything west of Selwood went to the new see of Sherborne. In around 900, it was reduced to Hampshire and Surrey when Edward the Elder removed Berkshire and Wiltshire, which had also been part of the original diocese, and transferred them to the new diocese of Ramsbury. The creation of the new dioceses of Guildford and Portsmouth in 1927 reduced Winchester further.

Today the diocese of Winchester is roughly coterminous with west and central Hampshire, two-thirds of the county in an area including Southampton, but excluding Portsmouth, the area immediately to its north and a few parishes in the north-east. The diocese also includes most of Bournemouth, which was historically part of Hampshire until it became part of Dorset with the reorganisation of local government in 1974. Also included in the diocese are the Channel Islands, which were originally part of the diocese of Coutances in France until they were placed under the episcopal jurisdiction of Winchester in 1569.

Two Venerable Buildings

Is **The Old Blue Boar** the oldest house in Winchester? Many people believe it is. It is likely that the former inn, now a private house, dates back to the fourteenth century. Standing on the corner of Blue Ball Hill and St John's Street, it has survived everything that the centuries have thrown at it. The Winchester City Trust's 1969 annual report highlighted the building's parlous state:

> *This old inn has been derelict for some time. Just as work was about to begin on the restoration some years ago, a huge mobile crane crashed into the upper floor and made the task even more difficult. Members of the Trust will be glad to learn that work is to begin shortly and that the missing timbers were taken away, stored, and will be used again.*

The **Chesil Rectory** is another of Winchester's ancient gems. Currently a popular restaurant, it was built by a wealthy merchant in the first half of the fifteenth century. Believed to be the oldest commercial property in Winchester, it is further distinguished by its state of repair, as most of the front of the building is original. One noted previous owner was Henry VIII who gave it to his daughter Mary, who then gave it to the city in which she married.

WINCHESTER PLACES

Winchester College

One of the oldest public schools in the country, **Winchester College** is also regarded as one of the very finest. When Henry VI founded Eton College, he took Winchester as his model – a tribute to the remarkable William of Wykeham, who founded Winchester College in 1382, setting in train more than 600 years of unbroken history which have shaped some of our finest minds. Politicians, writers, artists, sportsmen, scientists and leaders of industry have all been proud to count themselves Wykehamists, the word which has entered the *Oxford Dictionary of Phrase and Fable* to denote a past or present member of Winchester College.

Twentieth-century alumni include: Douglas Jardine, cricketer; Cecil Harmsworth King, newspaper publisher; Anthony Asquith, film director; John Snagge, BBC announcer; Hugh Gaitskell, leader of the Labour Party; Richard Crossman, Labour politician and diarist; Nicholas Monsarrat, author of *The Cruel Sea*; Kenneth Clark, art historian and broadcaster; Willie Whitelaw, politician; M. R. D. Foot, historian; Geoffrey Warnock, philosopher and academic; Geoffrey Howe, Lord Howe of Aberavon, politician; Alasdair Milne, BBC Director-General; Reginald Bosanquet, ITN newscaster; Tim Brooke-Taylor, comedian; and Antony Beevor, historian.

Winchester College comes complete with its own slang and vocabulary known as 'notions'. 'Short Half' is the first (autumn) term; 'Common Time', the second (Easter) term; 'Cloister Time', the third (summer) term; and 'Win: Coll:', Winchester College itself.

Three Oxford colleges owe their foundation to three different bishops of Winchester.

William of Wykeham, Bishop of Winchester from 1366 to 1404, was the founder of New College, Oxford (1379).

William Waynflete (*c.*1398–1486), Bishop of Winchester from 1447 to 1486, was the founder of Magdalen College, Oxford (1458).

And **Richard Fox or Foxe** (1447/8–1528), Bishop of Winchester from 1501 to 1528, was the founder of Corpus Christi College, Oxford (1517).

United in Death

Cardinal Henry Beaufort (*c.*1374–1447) was one of the most powerful of Winchester's bishops (1404 to 1447). A key political figure under the reigns of Henrys IV, V and VI, he held huge sway and effectively governed the country, and yet it is for his role in the trial and condemnation of **Joan of Arc** that he is most remembered today.

Paul Delaroche's celebrated painting *Beaufort and Joan of Arc* shows a stern, almost vicious-looking Beaufort interrogating a distinctly saintly-looking Joan of Arc in a murky prison, with a scribe lurking, pen poised, in the half-lit background. Cowered but undefeated, Joan beams purity and resolve. In his angry red robes, Beaufort is a glowering, menacing presence, his jabbing finger momentarily relaxed, waiting its moment to accuse again.

It's ironic that the two are commemorated together in Winchester Cathedral. Just a few yards from Beaufort's ornate tomb is a statue of Joan which was unveiled on 30 May 1923 as an act of national reconciliation, just a few years after her canonisation.

WINCHESTER CULTURE

Significant Organists

Winchester Cathedral helped make Winchester an important centre of learning. It also made it a centre of musical excellence.

Adrian Batten (1591-1637) was a chorister and organ scholar at Winchester Cathedral. He wrote several services and more than fifty anthems, but his name lives on principally in the 498-page *Batten Organbook* which saved for posterity a significant collection of contemporary church music. Some scholars insist it is in his own hand; others insist that it cannot safely be attributed to him. But none of them doubt the significance of the works it has preserved.

Despite his tendency to bouts of drinking and outrageous behaviour, **Thomas Weelkes** (*c*.1575–1623) was appointed organist at Winchester College in 1598 and then at Chichester Cathedral in around 1601, where he proved somewhat less than assiduous in his attendance at services. His behaviour deteriorated, and one story has him urinating on the dean from the organ loft during evensong. Eventually, he was dismissed for drunkenness and profanity. Weelkes' more lasting reputation, however, is as one of his era's most prolific and important composers of madrigals, of which nearly a hundred survive. His Winchester years resulted in two volumes of madrigals, the first in 1598, the second in 1600.

John Reading seems to have been rather a forbidding figure. After less than a year as organist and master of the choristers at Chichester Cathedral, he took up the corresponding post at Winchester Cathedral in 1675 where he was reprimanded for his 'undue and over severe correction to some of the Choristers'. He moved on to become organist at Winchester College (1681–1692) where he composed the college song 'Dulce Domum'.

Composer and organist **Richard Ayleward** (1626–1669) was born in Winchester and was a chorister at the cathedral. Towards the end of his life, he was organist and master of the choristers at Norwich Cathedral where he is buried. His legacy is at least three services and twenty-five anthems, among them 'The King shall Rejoice' to mark the coronation of Charles II in 1661.

Born in Winchester, **William King** (1624–1680) became organist at New College, Oxford. He composed services, anthems and a volume of poetry. His most popular anthems included 'O Be Joyful in God' and 'The Lord is King'. He died at New College on 7 November 1680 where he was buried in the cloisters. His tombstone carries the epitaph 'his singular eminence in music made him a partaker of the consort of angels'.

Organist and composer (1674–1707) **Jeremiah Clarke** was appointed organist at Winchester College in 1692. His works include 'Come, Come Along for a Dance and a Song' which was first performed in 1696. He also wrote a good deal of music for the London theatres and is believed to have been music master to Queen Anne. Prone to depression, he shot himself in the head on 1 December 1707 and was buried in the crypt of St Paul's Cathedral.

Daniel Roseingrave (*c.*1655–1727) was organist at Winchester Cathedral from 1681 to 1692 and later organist and vicar-choral at St Patrick's Cathedral, Dublin. He is known for the anthems 'Lord, Thou Art Become Gracious' and 'Haste Thee, O God', but otherwise few of his works have survived. His son and pupil, the organist and composer **Thomas Roseingrave** (*c.*1690–1766), was born in Winchester though he spent his early years in Ireland and died at Dún Laoghaire in 1766. Appointed organist at St George's, Hanover Square, Thomas wrote pieces including operas and cantatas.

George Benjamin Arnold (1832–1902) was organist at Winchester Cathedral from 1865 until his death, and he was buried there. His compositions include the oratorio *Ahab* (1864) and the sacred cantata *Sennacherib* (1883). His *Orchestral Introduction and Chorus in Praise of King Alfred* was performed at the inauguration of Alfred's statue in 1901.

Composer and conductor **Samuel Sebastian Wesley** (1810–1876) was organist at Hereford Cathedral (1832–1835), Exeter Cathedral (1835–1841), Winchester Cathedral (1849–1865) and Gloucester

Cathedral (1865–1876). His compositions include the anthem 'Thou Wilt Keep Him in Perfect Peace'.

Charles Dibdin (1745–1814) was a dramatist, entrepreneur, composer, actor and writer, best known as the composer of 'Poor Tom Bowling', which often features at the Last Night of the Proms. Dibdin's father died when he was young, and the family moved to Winchester where Charles became a chorister at Winchester Cathedral. His first work was the operetta *The Shepherd's Artifice* (1764). For many, his reputation rests on his ballads and sea songs. The politician Michael Heseltine, who has the middle name Dibdin, is a four times great-grandson.

Winchester's Butter Cross

If you want to go your separate ways on a Saturday afternoon shopping trip to Winchester, the chances are that you will arrange to meet up again at the **Butter Cross** in the High Street. It remains today, just as it has always been, the city's great meeting point. A scheduled ancient monument, originally called the High Cross, it offers a remarkable fifteenth-century flourish amid the bustle of modern Winchester. It is strange then to reflect how close the city came to losing it altogether.

In 1770 the Corporation of Winchester sold it to one Thomas Dummer whose intention was to dismantle it and have it re-erected at Cranbury Park, near Otterbourne. The people of Winchester decided otherwise and organised a riot to meet Dummer's workmen. The Corporation backed down; Dummer was forced to erect a facsimile at Cranbury Park

which didn't last long; and Winchester retained its Cross. A century later, in 1865, it was properly restored by G. G. Scott.

Over the years, the High Cross has become known as the Butter Cross, and there are a couple of possible reasons why. One is that it was the only place the good citizens of Winchester were permitted to eat butter during Lent. Much more likely is the suggestion that the name stuck because it was here that local farmers sold butter.

Standing on an octagonal base carved into five steps, the cross features statues of kings and saints. Each of the four faces of the monument has a large figure half way up, with two smaller figures in niches. Sketched by Joseph Mallord William Turner in 1795, it stands 43 foot high.

Men of Science and Learning

Alfred the Great inaugurated a tradition of Winchester scholarship which many were happy to uphold.

Physician **Walter Bayley** (1529–1593), who studied at Winchester College and New College, Oxford, rose to become regius professor of physic (medicine) at Oxford in 1561 and one of the physicians to Elizabeth I. His works include *A Brief Treatise Touching the Preservation of the Eyesight* (1586) and *A Short Discourse of the Three Kinds of Pepper in Common Use* (1588).

Born in Winchester and educated at Winchester College, **John Betts** (*c.*1623–1695) became a fellow of the College of Physicians in 1664. Practising in London, he was appointed Physician-in-Ordinary to Charles II. His works included a treatise on blood, *De ortu et natura sanguinis* (1669).

Chart-maker **William Hack** (*fl.* 1671–1702), the son of a Winchester innkeeper, studied in London and worked mainly on the production of paper charts bound into atlases. His big moment came in 1682 when he was secretly commissioned to copy a book of charts seized off modern Ecuador, a chance he leapt at, producing a lavish presentation copy for Charles II. His output was prolific, at the very least 300 charts in just twenty years, a reflection of a thriving industry in an era of maritime expansion.

Naturalist **John Latham** (1740–1837) practised medicine in Dartford for thirty-five years, but his real passion was natural history, in particular ornithology and comparative anatomy. His works included *A General Synopsis of Birds* (1781–1785), which was later enlarged and appeared in ten volumes as *A General History of Birds* (1821–1828), by which time Latham had moved to Winchester to live with his daughter and her husband. He died in the city and was buried in Romsey Abbey.

Born in Scotland, the physician **James Carmichael Smyth** (1742–1821) set up practice in London and was appointed physician to the Middlesex Hospital in 1775. Jail fever (typhus) was a particular interest, and he investigated nitrous acid gas as a means of preventing contagion. An epidemic of typhus at both Winchester prison and hospital brought him to the city to continue his experiments, at the invitation of the government.

A Man of Wealth and Taste

Peter Symonds College in Winchester is one of the largest sixth-form colleges in Britain, boasting more than 3,000 students. Originally founded as a boys' school in 1897, the site became a co-educational sixth-form college in 1974. However, its roots go back to the sixteenth century and the celebrated merchant who gave the establishment its name. Through the charities he established, Peter Symonds made the foundation of the school possible more than 300 years after his death.

Born into an important Winchester family, Symonds (*c.*1528–1586/7) was probably twelve or thirteen when his father sent him to London to work, but he kept close links with his home town throughout his life. In the capital, he became a successful mercer, rising to become one of the wardens of the Mercers' Company. The cloth trade made him a rich man, but his primary concern wasn't spending money in his lifetime. Symonds acquired land but worked on a detailed will which specified what was to be done with his possessions after his death.

One of his bequests was to fund an Easter sermon in the church of St Mary Kalender (or Kalendar), Winchester; another was for the provision of bread for the poor at a variety of locations; but most significant of all was his instruction that after his wife's death, most of his wealth should go towards setting up Christ's Hospital, an almshouse in Winchester for six poor men and four poor boys. The almshouse still survives in Symonds Street, but it has long since been overshadowed by a consequence of his generosity he never intended. When Symonds' endowment rose in value in the nineteenth century, it was decided to use some of the money to set up a boys' school in the city – the present Peter Symonds College.

A Royal Wedding

Mary I's wedding to **Philip II of Spain** in Winchester Cathedral on 25 July 1554 must rank as one of the most remarkable events ever staged there. Thousands crammed into a cathedral richly decorated with golden cloth. On a scaffold erected specially for the occasion, the couple sat – two days after they first met. The pomp of the day was matched only by the difficulties of protocol it created. Husband he might be, but equal he was not. At the wedding banquet, Philip was served on silver; Queen Mary was served on gold.

In other respects, however, he held the upper hand. Marriage for Mary was all about producing a Catholic successor. She was short and plump; contemporary accounts are hardly gracious, remarking on her age and general flabbiness. Philip, on the other hand, was younger, sexually more experienced and – according to commentators – had handsome legs.

The wedding, for all its splendour, proved of little benefit to Winchester. After its Saxon heyday and its Norman majesty, it was no longer a key seat of power and was generally a city in decline as the sixteenth century progressed.

Other notable royal occasions in the cathedral include Henry III's baptism in 1207 and Prince Arthur's baptism in 1486. Henry IV married Joan of Navarre in the cathedral in 1403.

Winchester's Writers

Part of Winchester's cultural wealth has long been the inspiration it has offered to writers.

Gloucestershire-born Parliamentarian officer and poet **John Ward** (*c.*1599–*c.*1658) voiced his support for the Roundhead cause at the outbreak of the English Civil War. In December 1642, he took part in the storming of Winchester under the command of Sir William Waller, an event he recorded in the poem *The Taking* of *Winchester by the Parliaments Forces.*

Poet **Thomas Fletcher** (1666–1713) was born in Avington, near Winchester, and educated at Winchester College. He was the author of *Poems on several occasions and translations, wherein the first and second books of Virgil's Æneis are attempted in English* (1692). He became under-master of Winchester College in 1701 and a fellow in 1711; he died in 1713 and was buried in Winchester Cathedral.

Biblical critic and writer **Robert Lowth** (1710–1787) was born in the Cathedral Close in Winchester and attended Winchester College. His early writings included an elegy on the fates of Charles I and the city during the English Civil War. He was elected professor of poetry at Oxford in 1741. He became a priest in 1742 and Archdeacon of Winchester in 1750.

Welsh-born poet **Jane Cave** (*b.* 1754/5, *d.* in or before 1813) moved to Winchester in 1779 where she published, four years later, *Poems on Various Subjects, Entertaining, Elegiac, and Religious.*

Roman Catholic priest and historian **John Lingard** (1771–1851) was born in Winchester. His reputation rests on his eight-volume work, *The History of England, From the First Invasion by the Romans to the Accession of Henry VIII* (1819–1830). He was also the author of *The Antiquities of the Anglo-Saxon Church* (1806).

Gone Fishing!

Izaak Walton (1593–1683) savoured the art and the spirit of fishing, and celebrated them both in his most famous work of poetry and prose, *The Compleat Angler* (1653).

The volume has gone through more than 400 editions since it first appeared, but in his own lifetime Walton was apparently better known for his lives of John Donne (1640), Henry Wotton (1651), Richard Hooker (1665), George Herbert (1670) and Robert Sanderson (1678), impressive works which in the eyes of some make him the father of modern biography. However, it is on the enduring success of *The Compleat Angler* that his reputation now rests. With its celebrated epigraph 'Study to be quiet', the book is firmly in the pastoral tradition, weaving together practical information and folklore, songs and ballads to create enticing glimpses of a rural idyll.

Walton spent his last years in Winchester, living with his son-in-law Prebendary Hawkins at 7 The Close. He died in the city on 15 December 1683 and was buried in Prior Silkstede's Chapel in the south transept of Winchester Cathedral. In 1914, the fishermen of England and America combined to fund a memorial window in the chapel. Inevitably, it shows him fishing on the Itchen.

Walton wasn't Winchester's only famous angler. **George Selwyn Marryat** (1840–1896) was born in Milton, Hampshire, but developed his love of fly-fishing on the River Frome when his family moved to Dorset – a love he transferred back to Hampshire when he became a student at Winchester College (1854–1857). The River Itchen became a favourite haunt, and, after service in the army and a spell in Australia, he returned to Hampshire once again in 1874. Settling in Shedfield, just south of Winchester, he fished on the River Test, teaming up with Frederic Michael Halford to produce *Floating Flies and How to Dress Them* (1886) and *Dry Fly Fishing in Theory and Practice* (1889).

Angler and writer on fly-fishing **George Edward Mackenzie Skues** (1858–1949) was born in St John's, Newfoundland, and studied at Winchester College, where, just as it had with Marryat before him, the River Itchen proved a major attraction – and inspired a career which was to make him arguably the finest all-round fly-fisherman and writer on fly-fishing of the twentieth century. His books included *Minor Tactics of the Chalk Stream*

(1910) and *The Way of a Trout with a Fly* (1921). Following his death, his ashes were scattered on the banks of his beloved Itchen.

Civil War Destruction and Desecration

The **English Civil War** brought something of a conflict of interests for Parliamentarian army officer Sir William Waller who ended up sacking his own city.

In 1638, Sir William acquired Winchester Castle and set about repairing it. Four years later, he found himself advancing towards Winchester in the Parliamentarian cause as Civil War raged. After summer success besieging Royalist Portsmouth, he took Farnham Castle on 1 December 1642 and followed up by taking Winchester on 12 December. The castle surrendered; Waller's men wanted to sack the town, and he let them. In Chichester also, the Roundheads attacked the cathedral, smashing windows and scattering bones.

Winchester was regained by the Royalists, but eventually Cromwell held sway and ordered the destruction of the castle's fortifications. All that remained was granted back to Waller, but even then, the castle was still considered a potential threat. The order was put out 'to consider how Winchester Castle may be made untenable so that no damage may arise thereby and how satisfaction may be made to Sir William Waller for such damage as he shall sustain by reason thereof'. Demolition began, but proceeded slowly; it was gone, however, by the time Charles II conceived his palace on the site in the 1680s.

Education and Educators

Winchester College senior mathematical master **Clement Vavasor Durell** (1882–1968) became known to the world as a prolific writer of maths textbooks. It was said that there were few schools in the English-speaking world he did not reach. His most notable work was in the 1920s and 1930s with the Mathematical Association's publisher, G. Bell & Sons. His *General Arithmetic*, first published in 1936, became an international bestseller.

Dame Myra Curtis (1886–1971) was educated at Winchester School for Girls. She was appointed in 1945 by Home Secretary Herbert Morrison to chair a committee investigating the 'care of children deprived of a normal home life' in England and

Wales. Under her direction, the Care of Children Committee's work led to the Children's Act of 1948, which made the care of homeless or deprived children ultimately a Home Office responsibility.

Sir Walter Fraser Oakeshott (1903–1987), schoolmaster and college head, joined the staff at Winchester College in 1931, where he remained until 1938. In 1934 he discovered the manuscript of *Le Morte Darthur* by Sir Thomas Malory in the Fellows' Library. He is also remembered for his two studies of the Winchester Bible: *The Artists of the Winchester Bible* (1945) and *The Two Winchester Bibles* (1981).

Educationist **Robert Beloe** (1905–1984) was born in Winchester and educated at Winchester College. In 1958, he was chairman of a committee charged with reviewing school examinations. The Beloe Report of 1960 led to the introduction five years later of the Certificate of Secondary Education (CSE) as an alternative to the GCE. In 1988 GCEs and CSEs were merged to become GCSEs.

Dreaming of Versailles

It was a bold dream; one can't help but wonder just how different the city would have been had it come to pass. **Charles II** (1630–1685) decided that he wanted an English Versailles and he wanted it at Winchester, on the site of William the Conqueror's castle which had been virtually demolished during the English Civil War that killed his father.

Charles, who had been restored to the throne in 1660, determined that Sir Christopher Wren was the man to deliver his dream, a narrowing sequence of courts in direct imitation of the great French palace. The aim was to create a new autumn residence for the court, and in late 1682 work began. Charles was impatient, and progress was rapid. Remarkably, most of the construction work was finished by 1685, but with Charles' death that year, the scheme foundered. The project was abandoned by his successor James

II and never resumed. For a while, there were hopes that Queen Anne might revive the palace dream, but they remained unfulfilled.

The building, known as the King's House, fell into neglect, finally finding a use as a depot for prisoners of war during the Seven Years' War and then later during the War of American Independence. When revolution engulfed Paris, the site became an asylum for France's refugee clergy. It was then taken over by the military.

Officers' quarters and a military hospital were added, as were barrack accommodation for married soldiers, a school room and stores. In 1872, the barracks was officially titled The Rifle Depot, but disaster struck in December 1894 when the original King's House was destroyed by fire. It was rebuilt in Wren's style and reopened in 1904. During World War One, the site was an important mobilisation point; during World War Two, it served a similar purpose, also serving as a base for US soldiers preparing to take part in D-Day.

After the war, it was variously the Green Jackets Depot (1951–1958); the Green Jackets Brigade Depot (1959–1965); the Rifle Depot (1966–1982); and the Light Division Depot (Winchester) (1983–1986), at which point its use as a training depot ceased. In 1994, the Ministry of Defence released most of the site for private residential use. The central area has now been attractively landscaped under the name Peninsula Square. Close by, a statue honours field marshal Sir John Colborne, first Baron Seaton (1778–1863), commander of the 52nd Light Infantry during the Peninsular War and at the Battle of Waterloo.

Part of the site is now home to the regimental headquarters of the Royal Green Jackets; another part houses Winchester's military museums. The military museums comprise five separate museums: HorsePower, the Regimental Museum of the King's Royal Hussars; Light Infantry Museum; the Royal Green Jackets (Rifles) Museum; the Gurkha Museum; and the Guardroom Museum, the Museum of the Adjutant-General's Corps. The museums offer themselves as 'probably one of the most significant collections of military history outside London'. Nearby is a sixth museum, the Royal Hampshire Regiment Museum in Serle's House on Southgate Street.

Also nearby is the former barracks chapel, now the Everyman Winchester cinema, a highly successful conversion which has transformed the grade II listed building into a stylish, modern picture house where you can watch blockbusters in a building which retains the nineteenth-century charm of wooden beams and dressed stone walls. It was opened in February 1996 by Emma Thompson with her film version of Jane Austen's *Sense and Sensibility*.

As the scenes came back to me one by one, the same sensation of dreamy unnatural oppression came over me so strongly that I stopped writing, and said to Miss Lamont, 'Do you think that the Petit Trianon is haunted?'

AN ADVENTURE, ELIZABETH MORISON AND
FRANCES LAMONT (MACMILLAN, 1911)

Born in Winchester, the daughter of the headmaster of Winchester College, **Charlotte Anne Elizabeth Moberly** (1846–1937), was a distinguished academic who rose to become the first principal of St Hugh's College, Oxford. However, if she is remembered at all, it is for what may or may not have happened just outside Paris one August day in 1901. While visiting the Palace of Versailles, she and her friend and fellow academic Eleanor Jourdain somehow managed to slip back in time to the days of Marie Antoinette. After becoming lost, they found themselves in what felt like a *tableau vivant* or living picture of the eighteenth century. When Moberly and Jourdain researched it all later, they became convinced that they had seen the doomed queen herself in person. Under the pseudonyms Elizabeth Morison and Frances Lamont, they turned their story into the rather vaguely titled bestseller *An Adventure*, prompting plenty of derision but also a significant amount of genuine curiosity.

The Great Humanitarians

Among Winchester's proudest tradition is the strong sense of justice which has made it home to people to keen to improve the lot of their fellow men.

Josephine Butler College, Durham University's youngest college, opened in 2006 and declares itself free-spirited, flourishing and full of life. As the prospectus explains: 'We are named after the nineteenth-century social reformer, **Josephine Butler**, who had a profound influence on society's view of women's health and education.' The fact that the college is in Durham reflects Butler's Northumberland birth, but Winchester can also lay

claim to her. Née Grey, she married George Butler, an academic who became Dean of Winchester, in 1852. Butler (1828–1906) campaigned vigorously against child prostitution; she also campaigned against the Contagious Diseases Acts, which permitted the police to arrest women living in seaports and military towns whom they believed were prostitutes and compel them to be examined for venereal disease. In 1883, the Acts were suspended and then later repealed.

Mary Elizabeth Sumner (1828–1921) was married to George Henry Sumner, son of the Bishop of Winchester. At first they lived in Crawley, five miles north-west of Winchester, then Farnham Castle and Old Alresford, but when her husband became an archdeacon, they moved to Winchester Cathedral Close where they remained. Here Mary developed her ideas for a network of mothers' groups based on Bible reading, prayer and fellowship, and founded the Mothers' Union as a result. By the time of her death, it had spread countrywide.

Ellen Joyce (1832–1924), who lived at St John's Croft, Winchester, was devoted to the cause of women and Empire. She was adamant that the emigration of fine British women was a vital part of maintaining and extending Britain's global pre-eminence. She saw benefits for the women themselves in terms of the opportunities emigration brought them, but more importantly saw it as a key way to further a strong, pure and Christianising British Empire.

Rebecca Strong (1843–1944) trained as a nurse at St Thomas' Hospital, London, at Winchester Hospital and at the new British army hospital at Netley, Southampton. Appointed matron at the Glasgow Royal Infirmary, she was appalled by the low quality of nursing care. The experience convinced her that it was not enough to train nurses on the wards; they needed proper lectures and examinations. After several years running her own private nursing home, she returned to the Glasgow Royal Infirmary to put her new scheme into practice in 1893, setting standards which continue today.

Rebecca Jarrett (1846–1928) knew how hard life could be; she was the youngest of thirteen children with an absent father and a drunken mother who tried to force her into prostitution. For 20 years, Rebecca moved around the country, living off men, until 1884 when she collapsed outside a Salvation Army hostel in Northampton. Her good fortune was that she fell into the care of someone determined to save her from the demon drink. Jarrett recovered at the Whitechapel Hospital in London and was sent to seek sanctuary in Winchester with Josephine Butler. She later helped the fallen women of Portsmouth and, with the help of the Butlers, set up her own refuge at Hope Cottage, Winchester.

One of the first British psychiatric nurses of national standing, **Eileen Skellern** (1923–1980) made an important contribution to the development of modern mental health nursing. One of her last acts was the planning of the First International Psychiatric Nursing Congress in 1980, which took place in London two months after her death. Skellern advised the Home Office on nursing in the prison service and laid the groundwork for the 1972 White Paper *Better Services for the Mentally Handicapped*. Her struggle against cancer forced her into early retirement, and she died at her home in Alresford Road, Winchester.

WINCHESTER PLACES

Abbey House

The mayoralty of Winchester is one of the oldest in the country, dating back to the days when the city was the capital of England. There have been more than 800 mayors of Winchester, and it is one of just five cities in the country to have an official residence for its mayor. Built in about 1700, the **Abbey House** is a substantial town house standing in the attractive Abbey Gardens, just off The Broadway on the site of a monastic establishment known as Nunnaminster and later St Mary's Abbey. The Abbey was destroyed during the dissolution of the monasteries under Henry VIII.

Abbey House was built by the Recorder of Winchester, William Pescod, and was bought by the City Council in 1889. Since then, the grounds have been open to the public and the house has been available to the mayor.

Winchester Lends its Name

Winchester ware is a late Saxon style of earthenware pottery typical of the period (AD 850–1150). A yellowish-red or green-coloured glaze is common, and the range of vessel types includes pitchers, jars, cups, bowls and bottles.

Originating in Winchester in the tenth and eleventh centuries, the **Winchester School** of calligraphy and manuscript illumination was the finest in Europe. In late Saxon times, during the century before the Norman Conquest, Winchester was the artistic capital of England. The school's most distinctive characteristic is the use of bold, leafy borders around miniatures.

The **Winchester Bible**, the finest of all surviving twelfth-century English bibles and the work of a single scribe, was commissioned in 1160, probably by Bishop Henry de Blois. Designed for ceremonial use rather than individual study, it can be viewed in Winchester Cathedral.

The **Winchester measure** is a set of legal standards of volume introduced by Henry VII in the late fifteenth century. The measures comprise the **Winchester bushel**, the peck, the gallon and the quart.

The **Winchester disk** is an obsolete type of small, high-capacity computer disk.

Winchester fives is a game of hand-ball played by pairs on a three-walled court, similar to squash but without rackets, the ball being played by the palm of the hand. The game dates back to Tudor times, but its modern form derives from versions played at Eton, Rugby and Winchester.

The **Winchester rifle** is a breech-loading side-action repeating rifle, named after its American manufacturer, Oliver F. Winchester (1810–1880). It was also one of many types of rifle used by the Cheyenne and Sioux at Little Bighorn, the battle at which General George Custer and all the men with him were killed in 1876.

Winchester syndrome is a rare congenital connective tissue disease which results in short stature and marked contractures of the joints.

The **Winchester bottle** is a large, strong, cylindrical bottle used particularly in the pharmaceutical and chemical industries.

The **Winchester knot** is a particular way of tying a
tie. Offering a wide and thick knot, it is regarded as
particularly suitable for men with long necks.

A Statue to Good Queen Anne

In Winchester, as in any historic city, it's worth looking up. Winchester's shopping streets are dominated by many of the shopping chains you will find almost anywhere; but at first-floor level, you can still see much that is unique to the city. In fact, the more you look up, the more you find – evidence of past times and past uses. Among the many treasures is a statue of **Queen Anne** (1665–1714) above Lloyds Bank, on the south side of the High Street.

The building was the city's guildhall from the time of Edward IV to James II, by which time it was in such a poor state of repair that it was decided to sell it off. The plan fell through, and instead the guildhall was rebuilt on the same site and remained in use until the present guildhall was opened in the nineteenth century. Standing on five Doric columns of stone, the upper portion is of brick with six fine windows facing the High Street.

In the middle is the statue of Queen Anne, given by George Bridges, MP for Winchester, above a tablet inscribed 'Anno Pacifico, Anna Regina 1713.' The statue marks her visit to Winchester in 1705, a time when it was fervently hoped that she might pick up where Charles II left off with his plans for a new royal palace in Winchester. She died a year after the statue was erected. Nearby, a richly carved bracket supports the town clock, presented by Sir William Paulet in 1713.

While the royal palace plan didn't progress, the eighteenth century was generally a good one for Winchester, with the century seeing the construction of many attractive houses and shops in the city. Many survive as fine examples of the period. Among them is the splendid Serle's House, now home to the Royal Hampshire Regiment Museum. Believed to be the work of architect Thomas Archer (1668-1743), it was built in about 1730 for William Sheldon. The Sheldon family remained there until 1781 when it was sold to lawyer James Serle. The house was sold to the government in 1796.

Winchester's Artists

With its cultural traditions and its natural advantages, it was inevitable that Winchester should prove the home or inspiration to numerous artists down the centuries.

John Plott (1732–1803), who was born and died in Winchester, was a painter of miniatures in Winchester and London and enjoyed success in both. Plott's portrait of his aunt *Mrs Lydia Butt* (1776) is in the collection at the Victoria and Albert Museum.

Nathaniel Dance (1735–1811) was a portrait painter whose commissions included George III, Captain James Cook and the actor David Garrick. He abandoned his artistic career in 1790 in favour of politics. The blessing is that at least he died happy, if rather unexpectedly. Dance was a guest in Kingsgate Street, Winchester, and was in full flow, describing to a party of ladies the 'absurdity' of some monuments recently placed in Winchester Cathedral, when he suddenly expired. The cathedral had the last laugh when he was buried there.

Charles Hayter (1761–1835) was a painter of miniatures who practised in London and Essex before moving to Winchester in 1832. His works include *An Introduction to Perspective, Adapted to the Capacities of Youth, in a Series of Pleasing and Familiar Dialogues* (1813) and *A New Practical Treatise on the Three Primitive Colours* (1826). Hayter was an early exponent of Thomas Young's 1802 theory that all colours could be mixed from the three primary ones – red, blue and yellow.

Engraver **Henry Chawner Shenton** (d. 1866) was baptised on 14 March 1803 at St Thomas' church, Winchester. His subjects were his contemporaries and also historical figures. Works included *James V, King of Scotland* (1834), *Olden Hospitality* (1846), *The Clemency of Coeur de Lion* (1856) and *A Labour for Love* (1863).

Music antiquarian and artist **Harry Ellis Wooldridge** (1845–1917) was born in the parish of St Lawrence in Winchester. He exhibited at the Royal Academy and also painted frescoes in St John's Church, Hampstead. Many regard as his finest work his reredos for St Martin's Church in Brighton. An authority on early music, he was responsible for a new edition of *William Chappell's Popular Music of the Olden Time*, under the new title *Old English Popular Music* (1893).

Sir Hamo Thornycroft (1850–1925) is the man we have to thank for Winchester's great emblem, the imposing statue of King Alfred erected in 1901 looking westwards towards the city centre from The Broadway. His other major works include *Oliver Cromwell* outside the Houses of Parliament, London (1899), *Gladstone* in the Strand, London (1905) and *Edward VII* in Karachi (1915), all in bronze.

Artist and archaeologist **George Heywood Maunoir Sumner** (1853–1940) was born in Old Alresford, Hampshire, the son of Mary Elizabeth Sumner, founder of the Mothers' Union. Sumner published two books of etchings, *The Itchen Valley* (1881) and *The Avon from Naseby to Tewkesbury* (1882), but also worked in a number of different media including textiles, tapestries and stained glass.

Regarded as the most influential artist in the New Sculpture movement, **Sir Alfred Gilbert** (1854–1934) created the fourteen-foot bronze statue of a seated Queen Victoria in Winchester's Great Hall. The piece was commissioned for Victoria's Golden Jubilee in May 1887, but it took 25 years to complete. Gilbert's masterpiece is generally considered to be the tomb of the Duke of Clarence (erected between 1892 and 1899, but not completed until 1928) in the Albert memorial chapel at Windsor Castle.

Known to millions for his humorous illustrations of ponies and horses, the cartoonist and illustrator **Norman Thelwell** (1923–2004) died at Bereweeke Court Nursing Home, Winchester. More than thirty collections of his cartoons were published in his lifetime including *Thelwell Country* (1959), *The Penguin Thelwell* (1963) and *The Compleat Tangler* (1967). He was a founder member of the British Cartoonists' Association in 1966.

British abstract painter **Gillian Ayres** (*b*. 1930) was head of painting at Winchester School of Art from 1978 to 1981. She then moved to Wales to devote herself full-time to painting.

WINCHESTER CULTURE

Jane Austen

One of the nation's most enduringly popular writers, sadly **Jane Austen** breathed her last in Winchester. Curiously, her tombstone in Winchester Cathedral gives no indication of her literary standing. It reads simply:

In Memory of
JANE AUSTEN
youngest daughter of the late
Revd GEORGE AUSTEN,
formerly Rector of Steventon in this County
she departed this Life on the 18th of July 1817,
aged 41, after a long illness supported with
the patience and the hopes of a Christian.

The benevolence of her heart,
the sweetness of her temper, and

the extraordinary endowments of her mind
obtained the regard of all who knew her, and
the warmest love of her intimate connections.

Their grief is in proportion to their affection
they know their loss to be irreparable
but in their deepest affliction they are consoled
by a firm though humble hope that her charity,
devotion, faith and purity have rendered
her soul acceptable in the sight of her
REDEEMER.

The memorial nearby records that she was 'known to many by her writings' – a discretion of which she would doubtless have approved.

Born in the rectory at Steventon, near Basingstoke, Austen (1775–1817) was the author of *Sense and Sensibility* (1811), *Pride and Prejudice* (1813), *Mansfield Park* (1814), *Emma* (1816) and the posthumously published *Northanger Abbey* and *Persuasion* (both 1818) – a remarkable output in a tragically short life.

In 1809, after a number of years in Bath, Jane moved with her mother and sisters to Chawton in Hampshire, where Jane wrote almost daily. *Mansfield Park*, *Emma*, and *Persuasion* were all written in the parlour at Chawton. However, by the summer of 1816, Austen's health was failing. It seems likely she was suffering from Addison's disease, a rare, chronic endocrine disorder.

There was no cure, and when her local apothecary admitted defeat, Austen moved to Winchester on 24 May 1817 under the care of Giles King Lyford, Surgeon-in-Ordinary at the city's County Hospital. Hopes initially rose. Three days after arriving in the city, she wrote to her nephew:

Mr Lyford says he will cure me, & if he fails I shall draw up a Memorial & lay it before the Dean and Chapter, & have no doubt of redress from that Pious, Learned & Disinterested Body.

Tragically, her optimism was ill-founded, and she died at 4.30 a.m. on 18 July at 8 College Street, where she was staying with her sister Cassandra. Her funeral was held in Winchester Cathedral at 8 a.m. on 24 July 1817.

On St Swithun's day 1817, three days before her death, she composed a comic poem from the saint to the people of Winchester, under its Latin name Venta, complaining about holding a race meeting on his day:

Oh! subjects rebellious!
Oh Venta depraved
When once we are buried
you think we are gone
But behold me immortal!
By vice you're enslaved
You have sinned and must suffer,
ten farther he said.

WINCHESTER PEOPLE

Sporting Prowess

Winchester has contributed to all fields of human endeavour, sport included.

Sussex-born cricketer **William Lillywhite** (1792–1854) became known as the Nonpareil Bowler, a key figure in the arguments surrounding the legalisation of round-arm bowling. 'I bowls the best ball in England,' he said. 'I suppose if I was to think every ball, they'd never get a run.' From 1851 to 1853 he was coach at Winchester School.

Cricketer **Betty Snowball** (1908–1988) trained as a physical education teacher and taught for many years at St Swithun's School, Winchester. Earlier, Snowball was a member of the first England women's side to tour abroad, travelling to Australia in 1934–1935 where she impressed as a wicketkeeper. She also impressed with the bat, scoring 613 runs in Test matches at an average of 40.86. Her greatest innings was 189 against New Zealand in 1935, a women's Test record for half a century.

Athlete and teacher of physical education **Geoffrey Harry George Dyson** (1914–1981) developed an interest in running when he joined the army. He showed promise as a hurdler, but instead took up a lectureship at the School of Athletic Games and Physical Education at Loughborough College in 1938. After the war, he was appointed the Amateur Athletic Association's first national athletics coach, remaining in position until 1961, after which he moved to Canada. Returning to the UK, he became the first director of physical training at Winchester College in 1970, where he stayed for six years.

Dyson's wife was the athlete and ballet teacher **Maureen Gardner** (1928–1974), a British champion hurdler who won a silver medal in the 80-metre hurdles at the 1948 Olympics in London at the age of nineteen. When Gardner and her husband returned from Canada in 1970, she set up a ballet school in Winchester. She died in Southampton after a long illness; a memorial service was held in the chapel at Winchester College.

Football legend **Terry Paine** made more than 800 appearances for Southampton Football Club in 18 seasons – a club record which still stands. He was born in Winchester on 23 March 1939 and played for Winchester City 1954–1956. Paine then played for Southampton 1957–1974, also making nineteen appearances for England between 1963 and 1966.

Nicknamed the 'Limestone Cowboy', darts player **Bob Anderson** was ranked world number one in the late 1980s. Born in Winchester on 7 November 1947, he scored his first darts maximum – three triple 20s – at the age of seven. He won the World Professional Championship in 1988 and the Winmau World Masters in 1986, 1987 and 1988.

Footballer **Wayne Bridge** was born in Southampton on 5 August 1980, but at an early age moved to Winchester where he attended Oliver's Battery Primary and Kings' School. It was while playing for Oliver's Battery that he was spotted and signed as a trainee at Southampton Football Club. He was with Southampton 1998–2003 before moving to Chelsea between 2003 and 2009. He has also played for Fulham, Manchester City, West Ham United, Sunderland and Brighton & Hove Albion, and played for England thirty-six times.

British freestyle swimmer **Julia Beckett** represented Great Britain at the 2008 Summer Olympics in the 4×100 m freestyle relay swimming event. The former Peter Symonds student was born in Winchester on 4 July 1986. Her father George Beckett was the leader of Winchester City Council.

Season of Mists and Mellow Fruitfulness

The English Romantic poet **John Keats** (1795–1821) famously said that Winchester's air was 'worth sixpence a pint'; tragically it did not do him much good. The tuberculosis which was to kill him was already with him when he stayed in the city with his friend Charles Armitage Brown from 12 August until early October 1819. A year and a half later, he was dead.

However, Keats' Winchester visit was to prove an inspirational one. He walked along the riverside path from Winchester College to the Hospital of St Cross one autumnal evening. *Ode to Autumn* was the result. Its opening lines are:

> *Season of mists and mellow fruitfulness,*
> *Close bosom-friend of the maturing sun;*
> *Conspiring with him how to load and bless*
> *With fruit the vines that round the*
> *thatch-eaves run*

While in the city, Keats also revised *The Eve of St Agnes*. Winchester was clearly a place which captured his imagination – and his affections. 'The side streets here are excessively maiden-lady-like', he wrote in a letter.

City Architects

A president of the Royal Institute of British Architects, **Sir William Tite** (1798–1873) was increasingly employed by the new railway companies in the 1840s. In this capacity, he designed many of the country's early railway stations, among them Winchester and Eastleigh.

Architect and draughtsman **Owen Browne Carter** (1806–1859) was the man who designed the Winchester Corn Exchange (1838), which now serves as the Winchester Discovery Centre, in other words its library. He also created the city's West Hill cemetery buildings (1840) and added a vestry at St Matthew's Church at nearby Weeke (1850).

One of the most prolific and original English Gothic Revivalists, architect and designer **William Butterfield** (1814–1900) designed the Royal Hampshire County Hospital in Winchester (1863–1864). The earlier Hampshire County Hospital, founded in 1736, was suffering drainage problems. A new hospital was needed on higher ground; Butterfield supplied the design, with Florence Nightingale offering advice. Queen Victoria joined in, contributing money to the appeal to fund it and also giving permission for it to be called Royal. By the nineteenth century Winchester was emerging as a popular place to which to retire, and the new hospital certainly added to its attractions. This also accounts perhaps for the fact that so many people associated with Winchester breathed their last there. The hospital was the major medical facility in the area.

In addition, Butterfield was the man behind significant restoration work at the Hospital of St Cross, also in Winchester (1864–1865).

Architect and author **Sir Herbert Baker** (1862–1946) produced war memorials for several schools following the 1914–1918 conflict. His masterpiece is considered by many to be the war memorial cloister at Winchester College (1922–1924). He described it as 'a work after my own heart, building in a manner which I loved in the architecture of my native country, flint and stone, oak roof-trees, all made living in expression with symbols, heraldry, and sculpture.'

I Predict a Riot

Joseph Mason (*b. c.*1799), a farm labourer living in the village of Bullington, just north of Winchester, and his brother **Robert Mason** (*b. c.*1806) came to the public's attention in the Captain Swing Riots of 1830 over the introduction of new threshing machines and subsequent loss of livelihoods. Popular protests spread across the south, with a number of parishes in open revolt.

In the backlash, the Mason brothers were charged by the Winchester special commission with 'demanding money' and sentenced to death. The sentences were commuted to transportation for life to New South Wales where, ironically, Joseph took the view that he was materially much better off than back home in Hampshire. Pardons were issued in the mid-1830s, but the Masons, along with most of the men they were transported with, seem to have opted to remain in Australia where they then disappeared from history.

Civil unrest was to hit Winchester once again less than a century later in May 1908, and for the most unlikely of reasons – the iron railings which surrounded a Russian gun which had been installed close to King Alfred's statue. The gun was a trophy from the Crimean War, and the area around it had subsequently become a popular meeting place.

A pageant was planned to raise funds for repairs to Winchester Cathedral, and in preparation, it was proposed to improve access to The Broadway. Part of the plan was to remove the railings around the gun, a plan which seemed innocuous enough, but it left local house-painter **Joe Dumper** incensed. He started a petition and organised a protest meeting.

Trouble was brewing, and when the authorities removed the railings anyway, trouble duly erupted. The following morning, more than 3,000 people, led by Dumper, gathered by the railing-less gun and went on the rampage, wrecking shop windows and street lights and even attacking the city clock. They also took out their fury on the props for the planned pageant. People power prevailed and the railings were restored – only for both gun and railings to be taken for scrap at the outbreak of World War Two thirty-one years later.

Winchester's Men and Women of God

Winchester's Christian traditions flourished in the Victorian age.

One of the most successful Christian missionaries of his age, **Thomas Birch Freeman** (1809–1890) was born in Twyford, near Winchester, possibly the son of a freed African slave. He volunteered as a Methodist missionary to West Africa and went on to found Methodist churches in the Gold Coast and Nigeria.

Henry Cadwallader Adams (1817–1899) was educated at Winchester College where he was later appointed as a master before becoming a priest. He was a prolific writer of works including religious commentaries, Greek and Latin grammars and historical tales, but his forte was as a writer of boys' school stories, among them *Schoolboy Honour* (1861). He also wrote a history of Winchester College, *Wykehamica* (1878).

The inscription on **Harriette McDougall's** memorial in Winchester Cathedral records simply that 'She first taught Christ to the women of Borneo'. McDougall (1818–1886) was born into a London family with evangelical missionary interests; and in turn she encouraged her husband Francis to apply for pioneer missionary work in Borneo. In all, they served in Sarawak for twenty years, losing five sons in six years – trying times chronicled in Harriette's two books *Letters from Sarawak: Addressed to a Child* (1854) and *Sketches of our Life at Sarawak* (1882).

After Christmas, we sailed in H.M.S. Amazon,
through the kindness of Captain Troubridge,
for Singapore, taking our child Harry with
us. [...] Soon after our arrival our little boy
died of diphtheria, leaving us childless, for
we had already lost two infants at Sarawak.
[...] Perhaps it urged us to a deeper interest in
the native people than we might have felt had
there been any little ones of our own to care
for; but those six years 'the flowers all died
along our way', one infant after another being
laid in God's acre.

SKETCHES OF OUR LIFE AT SARAWAK, CHAPTER
VII, THE LUNDUS

Back in England, Harriette and Francis worked in
Huntingdonshire, Ely and Winchester.

Henry Brougham Bousfield (1832–1902) was rector
of the parish of St Maurice with St Mary Kalender
and St Peter Colebrook, Winchester from 1861 to
1870, but missionary work was his guiding interest.
In 1878 he was consecrated Bishop of Pretoria in a

service at St Paul's Cathedral in London. On arrival in Pretoria, he found the church organisation was rudimentary, and it fell to Bousfield to pull together his new diocese, linking numerous isolated communities. He died suddenly of heart disease in Cape Town.

Dean of Winchester and ecclesiastical historian **William Richard Wood Stephens** (1839–1902) published widely, with collections including *Christianity and Islam, the Bible and the Koran: Four Lectures* (1877). He was also a noted biographer and writer on ecclesiastical history. Stephens was appointed Dean of Winchester in February 1895 and remained in post until his death from typhoid fever. He was buried in the graveyard of Winchester Cathedral.

Donald Coggan (1909–2000) was appointed Bishop of Bradford in 1956 and Archbishop of York in 1961 before being appointed the 101st Archbishop of Canterbury in 1974, a position he filled until his retirement in 1980 when he was created Baron Coggan. He moved first to Sissinghurst and then to Winchester where he built up a large following for his Lenten addresses. Coggan died at the Old Parsonage Nursing Home, Main Road, Otterbourne, near Winchester.

Church administrator **Dame (Mildred) Betty Ridley** (1909–2005) enjoyed a long and important role within the Church of England. She was vice-president of the British Council of Churches from 1954 to 1956, served on the central board of finance of the church assembly from 1955 to 1979 and was a church commissioner from 1959 to 1981. In 1972, she was appointed to be third church estates commissioner, the first woman to hold the post. Ridley was a lifelong supporter of the ordination of women. When the battle was finally won in 1992, Ridley, by now retired and living in Winchester, welcomed the news with tears of joy.

Derek Worlock (1920–1996) was born in London, but the family moved to Winchester in 1929 when his father became Conservative Party agent for the constituency. He was ordained to the priesthood in Westminster Cathedral in June 1944 and was appointed Roman Catholic Archbishop of Liverpool in 1976, remaining in the post until 1996.

The Theatre Royal Winchester

In common with so many theatres up and down the country, the **Theatre Royal Winchester** has had to navigate difficult times in its history. At one point, the building was nearly bulldozed off the map. But fortunately, the people of Winchester rallied behind it in its hour of need, and today the Theatre Royal finds itself in good health as an important cultural focus, offering a lively, wide-ranging programme of events.

The theatre stands in a building which was never intended to be a theatre. It began life in 1850 as the Market Hotel; it wasn't until the exciting new era of film that the building was used for entertainment purposes, opening as a cine variety theatre in 1914 and becoming a full-time cinema just after World War One.

When the cinema closed down in 1974, its owners wanted to demolish it – but the threatened destruction provoked an impassioned cry of support from the city. The Winchester Theatre Fund was set up to secure live theatre for the city. Money was raised, adjoining buildings were acquired, and the new theatre opened in 1978, becoming fully functional in 1981. The next chapter began in 1996 when the local authorities joined forces with local businesses and individual supporters to instigate five years of restoration and refurbishment, backed by the National Lottery. The theatre reopened in 2001.

The theatre stands in Jewry Street, a name which harks back to the early settlement of the Jews in Winchester and the welcome they received at a time when other cities were much less hospitable.

WINCHESTER CULTURE

Winchester's Musicians

The author of a World War One training pamphlet on grenade warfare, **Sir George Dyson** (1883–1964) was above all a composer and a music administrator. He was appointed director of music at Winchester College in 1924 and was later director of the Royal College of Music. Dyson wrote pieces for both the 1937 and 1953 coronation services. His most significant works include *The Canterbury Pilgrims*, first performed at Winchester in 1931, and *Belshazzar's Feast* (1935). A patron of the Winchester Music Club, he died at his home in the city at 1 St James Terrace.

Robert Irving (1913–1991), who was born and died in Winchester, was considered one of the world's finest modern ballet conductors. He was conductor and musical director of Sadler's Wells Ballet (1949–1958) and music director of the New York City Ballet (1958–1989). Irving was a student at Winchester College where there is now a plaque to his memory.

The Brook Brothers, often called the British Everly Brothers, released eight singles between 1960 and 1963 and toured with Cliff Richard before disappearing from the charts. Ricky Brook was born in Winchester on 24 October 1940; his brother Geoff Brook was born in the city on 12 April 1943.

Brian Eno is a musician, composer, record producer, singer and visual artist. Born 1948 in Woodbridge, Suffolk, he attended Ipswich Art School before studying at Winchester School of Art, graduating in 1969. He began his musical career with Roxy Music before making his own mark, most notably in the field of ambient music.

The English mezzo-soprano **Diana Montague** has enjoyed a distinguished career, with performances in many of the world's great opera houses and concert venues. She has performed major roles in operas by Bellini, Berlioz, Gluck, Mozart, Rossini and Strauss, among many others. She was born in Winchester in 1953.

One of the most respected British musicians of his generation, **Roger Steptoe** was born in Winchester in 1953. His chamber music, concertos, song cycles and instrumental sonatas have all been performed worldwide. As a pianist, he has particularly championed neglected British music. He is also highly regarded as a teacher. Since 1999, Steptoe has lived in Uzerche in the French Limousin.

Mat Flint has been a member of bands including Revolver, Hot Rod, Death in Vegas and Deep Cut. His family moved to Winchester when he was 16. Revolver drummer **Nick Dewey** was also from Winchester.

Singer-songwriter **Andy Burrows**, born in Winchester in 1979, was the drummer in the band Razorlight from 2004 to 2009, after which he joined We Are Scientists. His solo album *Company* was released in 2012.

The University of Winchester

The University of Winchester is one of the country's newest universities, established in 2005, but its educational roots go back the best part of two centuries. It began in 1840 as the Winchester Diocesan Training School, first in St Swithun's Street and then in the Bishop's Palace at Wolvesey before moving to a new building on its current site in 1862. It became King Alfred's College in 1928, the name by which it was known to generations. An accreditation agreement was signed with the University of Southampton in 1992. When the college was given degree-awarding powers in 2004, it was renamed University College Winchester before its relaunch as a university in its own right the following year.

WINCHESTER CULTURE

Winchester's Victorians Put Pen to Paper

George William Johnson (1802–1886) was appointed professor of moral and political economy at the Hindoo College in Calcutta in 1839. On his return, he wrote *The Stranger in India, or, Three Years in Calcutta* (1843) before settling in Winchester where he turned his attention to gardening. His works include *The Principles of Practical Gardening* (1845).

Schoolmaster **Charles Alexander Johns** (1811–1874) established himself in the 1840s as a popular author of works of natural history. In 1863 Johns and his wife set up Winton House, a private school in Winchester. A founder and first president of the Winchester Literary and Scientific Society, Johns continued to write, with works including *Rambles about Paris* (1859), *British Birds in their Haunts* (1862), and *Home Walks and Holiday Rambles* (1863). He died at Winton House and was buried at West Hill cemetery.

The prolific novelist **Charlotte Mary Yonge** (1823–1901) won a raft of admirers in her day including Lewis Carroll, George Eliot, Charles Kingsley, Christina Rossetti and Anthony Trollope, but she is little read in the twenty-first century. She was born at Otterbourne House, near Winchester, and brought up in a household devoted to the Church of England. John Keble, vicar of nearby Hursley and one of the leaders of the Oxford Movement, was an important influence on her novels. She is commemorated by the reredos in the Lady Chapel of Winchester Cathedral.

The antiquarian and travel writer **George Nelson Godwin** (1846–1907) was the son of a Winchester draper. He was educated at a private school in the city before being ordained a priest in 1870. One of the founder members of the Hampshire Field Club and Archaeological Society, he was also the first editor of *Hampshire Notes and Queries*. His major work was *Civil War in Hampshire, 1642–45, and the Story of Basing House* (1882).

Novelist and historian **Jessie Bedford** (1853–1918), who wrote under the name Elizabeth Godfrey, was born in Twyford and is believed to have spent much of her life in Winchester with her widowed mother, Emma. Her books include *Cornish Diamonds* (1895) and *The Winding Road* (1903). The conflict between marriage and career was a frequent theme in her writing. She also wrote on seventeenth-century history.

Ordained a deacon in 1887, **Claude Hermann Walter Johns** (1857–1920) became lecturer in Assyrian at King's College, London. His works include *Ancient Assyria* (1912), *A Survey of Recent Assyriology* (1914–1915) and *Ancient Babylonia* (1913) – despite never travelling to the Near East. Johns died at his home, Rathmines, Barnes Close, Winchester, and was buried nearby at Twyford.

William Holden Hutton (1860–1930) was born in Lincolnshire, studied at Magdalen College, Oxford, and became a fellow of St John's College, Oxford, until 1923. While there, he wrote a two-volume history of St John's (1891–8) and biographies of the Duke of Wellington (1893) and Thomas More (1895). He was appointed Dean of Winchester in 1919.

Ménie Muriel Dowie (1866–1945) secured her reputation as an adventurer with a six-month tour of the Carpathian Mountains in 1890, which resulted in the book *A Girl in the Karpathians*. Dowie and her husband bought Kitcombe Farm near Winchester in 1896, but the marriage ended in divorce soon after. She lived at Shepherd's Crown, near Winchester, in the 1930s before emigrating to America, where she died on 25 March 1945.

Naomi Gwladys Royde Smith (1875–1964) was the first female literary editor at the *Saturday Westminster Gazette*, in which she published early work by writers including Rupert Brooke, D. H. Lawrence and Graham Greene. Her first novel, regarded by many as her best, was *The Tortoiseshell Cat* (1925), which was followed by nearly forty more, several biographies and four plays. In the 1940s and 1950s, she lived in Winchester, in Colebrook Street and also for a while in Hyde Street.

London-born novelist **Ethel M. Dell** (1881–1939) originally wrote to amuse her friends. Her first novel

The Way of an Eagle (1912) was an instant hit, opening the floodgates for more than thirty novels and eight volumes of short stories. Romance and melodrama were key elements in tales in which strong virtue came face to face with outrageous villainy. After an operation for breast cancer, she moved with her husband from Ewhurst to Winchester in 1930. They later moved to Hertford, where she died in 1939, following a recurrence of her cancer.

The music critic and author **Francis Toye** (1883-1964) was born in Winchester and died in Florence where he had lived since 1946. Toye wrote for various English papers and journals, serving as music critic of *The Morning Post* from 1925 to 1937. His writings include books on Verdi (1931) and Rossini (1934).

WINCHESTER PLACES

The Guildhall

Opened in 1873, Winchester's **Guildhall** is one of the city's finest Victorian buildings. Constructed at a cost of £16,000, it stands on the site of St Mary's Abbey burial ground. Viscount Eversley laid the foundation stone in 1871, and two years later Lord Selborne officiated at the opening ceremony. Designed in the middle Gothic style, the Guildhall was built of Bath stone, and in its early years the building was very much at the centre of city activity. The *Victoria County History of Hampshire* (1912) notes that attached to the Guildhall were 'the police station, the fire station, the school of art and the public reading room and free library'. None are nearby now.

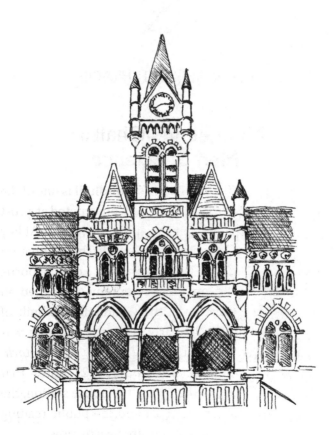

Nineteenth-Century Men of Science

The Victorian age was one of great scientific advances. Winchester played its part.

Medical writer **Robert Druitt** (1814–1883) spent four years as a pupil of his uncle, Charles Mayo, surgeon to the Winchester County Hospital, before setting up in general practice in London. His *Surgeon's Vade-Mecum* (1839) proved hugely popular and sold in tens of thousands, not just in the UK but also in the United States and in several European translations.

Army medical officer **Charles Mayo** (1837–1877) was born in Winchester, the elder son of Charles Mayo (1788–1876), senior surgeon at Winchester County Hospital. He studied at New College, Oxford, then travelled to the United States as staff surgeon-major and medical inspector to the 13th US Army Corps. The outbreak of the Franco-Prussian War in 1870 took him abroad again when he joined the medical service of the German army as staff surgeon-major and supervised the building of the Alice Hospital in Darmstadt.

The surveyor and geographer **Sir Charles Frederick Arden Close** (1865–1952) was a man who recognised the difficulties of waging war without maps. After precisely that experience in South Africa, he urged the preparation of maps for the likely theatre of war as World War One loomed. In August 1911, Close was appointed director-general of the Ordnance Survey. As a result of his efforts, Ordnance Survey printed 32 million maps for the armies in France and elsewhere during the 1914-1918 conflict. Close retired in 1922, but, standing in for staff away on military service, he taught mathematics at Winchester College during World War Two. He died at the Enniskerry Nursing Home, Sleepers Hill, Winchester.

Yorkshire-born aeronautical engineer **Sir Leonard Bairstow** (1880–1963) was appointed professor of aerodynamics at Imperial College, London in 1920 and was a member of what became the Aeronautical Research Council from 1921 to 1955, serving as its chairman from 1949 to 1952. His *Applied Aerodynamics* (1920) was for many years the definitive textbook. He died at the Royal Hampshire County Hospital in Winchester on 8 September 1963.

Lanarkshire-born physician and pathologist **Sir John William McNee** (1887–1984) laid the groundwork for our modern understanding of the functions of the liver. He was assistant adviser in pathology to the First Army in France during World War One and wrote significantly on gas poisoning, gas gangrene and trench fever. Throughout World War Two, McNee served as surgeon rear-admiral to the Royal Navy in Scotland and the Western Approaches. After his retirement, he and his wife Geraldine moved to Winchester where he became chairman of the Winchester district branch of the Council for the Protection of Rural England. He died at his home, Barton Edge, Worthy Road, Winchester.

Edinburgh-born meteorologist **Sir Charles William Blyth Normand** (1889–1982) combined his academic training with life as a meteorological officer in the army to observe the effects of the severe climate on his fellow soldiers. In 1927 he was appointed director-general of observatories in India. He left India in 1945 and served as secretary of the new International Ozone Commission from 1948 to 1959. A severe attack of bronchitis in 1959 prompted him to move to Winchester where he lived until his death in 1982.

Oxford-born archaeologist and librarian **(John) Nowell Linton Myres** (1902–1989) won a scholarship to Winchester College. With his friend Charles Stevens, he excavated St Catherine's Hill, Winchester. Other excavations followed, and in 1931 Myres was invited to contribute a section to *Roman Britain and the English Settlements* (1936), the first volume of the *Oxford History of England*. He served as librarian of Christ Church, Oxford before being appointed Bodley's librarian (the head of the Bodleian Library), a post he held for eighteen years.

(Charles Francis) Christopher Hawkes (1905–1992) studied at Winchester College and then at New College, Oxford, where he became increasingly interested in ancient history and archaeology. In 1925–1926 he returned to the city of his schooling to excavate the medieval chapel on St Catherine's Hill; in 1927–1928 this work was extended to its Iron Age hill fort.

The visionary computer technologist **Sir John Whitaker Fairclough** (1930–2003) took up a post with IBM in the United States in 1957 before returning to the UK a year later as director of development at IBM's newly established subsidiary, the Hursley laboratory near Winchester. After another spell in the USA, he returned to Hursley in 1974 as managing director. He later became director of manufacturing and development and chairman of IBM UK Laboratories Ltd.

The President of the Immortals Pays Winchester a Visit

The city of Wintoncester, that fine old city,
aforetime capital of Wessex, lay amidst its
convex and concave downlands in all the
brightness and warmth of a July morning.
TESS OF THE d'URBERVILLES,
THOMAS HARDY (1891)

In **Thomas Hardy's** fictionalised world of Wessex, Winchester became Wintoncester, and it was here that his tragic Tess, heroine of his great novel *Tess of the d'Urbervilles*, subtitled *A Pure Woman*, was executed for the murder of the dastardly Alec d'Urberville. The hapless Angel Clare and his sister-in-law Liza-Lu wait nearby:

Upon the cornice of the tower a tall staff was fixed. Their eyes were riveted on it. A few minutes after the hour had struck something moved slowly up the staff, and extended itself upon the breeze. It was a black flag. 'Justice' was done, and the President of the Immortals, in Aeschylean phrase, had ended his sport with Tess.

(*IBID*)

Thomas Hardy wasn't the only novelist to give Winchester a new name. **Anthony Trollope** (1815–1882) drew inspiration from both Winchester and Salisbury to create his Barchester. Born in London, Trollope was educated at Harrow and then at Winchester College, where to his embarrassment his bills were not paid. The cruelty of his fellow schoolboys completed his misery.

I suffered horribly! I could make no stand against it. I had no friend to whom I could pour out my sorrows. I was big, and awkward, and ugly, and, I have no doubt, skulked about

*in a most unattractive manner. Of course I
was ill-dressed and dirty. But, ah! how well I
remember all the agonies of my young heart;
how I considered whether I should always be
alone; whether I could not find my way up to
the top of that college tower, and from thence
put an end to everything?*

AN AUTOBIOGRAPHY,
ANTHONY TROLLOPE (1883)

Trollope was withdrawn from Winchester and
returned to Harrow, where he had an even more
wretched time. But at least school gave him the
chance to daydream, and, as he later wrote, if it had
not been for daydreaming, he would never have
written a novel.

A Giant among Judges

Alfred Thompson Denning, Baron Denning, (1899–1999) was a proud Hampshire man and one of the twentieth-century's most celebrated judges. Born in Whitchurch in the north of the county, Denning – known as Tom – studied at Magdalen College, Oxford, breaking off to serve with the Royal Engineers towards the end of World War One. After his graduation, he taught mathematics for a year in Winchester, where a visit to the assizes at Winchester Castle inspired him to enter the legal profession. Denning returned to Magdalen and gained a first in jurisprudence before proceeding to distinguish himself as a barrister. He was appointed Master of the Rolls in 1962, a position he held for twenty years. Lord Denning celebrated his one-hundredth birthday at his home in Whitchurch and died in Winchester's Royal Hampshire County Hospital just a few weeks later.

Denning was described in *The Times* as 'the best-known and best loved judge in our history' (18 June 1999). For *The Guardian*, he was 'the most celebrated English judge of the 20th century' (6 March 1999). Tony Blair, prime minister at the time of his death, commented: 'His judgments were a model of lucidity. He was prepared to use the law for its true purpose in the interests of fairness and justice. He had a tremendous feel for ordinary people.'

However, for many Denning remained a deeply controversial figure. Denning questioned the

suitability of some immigrants to act as jurors, and in 1982 at a trial arising out of the Bristol race riots he accused black defendants of using peremptory challenges to pack the jury with 'as many coloured people as possible'.

There was also outrage when he commented: 'We shouldn't have all these campaigns to get the Birmingham Six released if they'd been hanged. They'd have been forgotten and the whole community would have been satisfied.'

The six were sentenced to life imprisonment in 1975 for the Birmingham pub bombings – convictions which were later declared unsafe and quashed by the Court of Appeal.

WINCHESTER CULTURE

Winchester's Twentieth-Century Writers

Winchester's literary and scholarly traditions continued to flourish into the twentieth century. Winchester was once again proving an attractive place to live, particularly – given its wealth of facilities – in later life.

Educated at Winchester High School for Girls and at Newnham College, Cambridge, archaeologist and art historian **Jocelyn Mary Catherine Toynbee** (1897–1985) became a lecturer in classics at Cambridge where her particular interest was the culture of the Roman Empire. Her works include

Roman Medallions (1944) and *Art in Britain under the Romans* (1964).

Maurice Green (1906–1987) joined *The Daily Telegraph* as deputy editor in 1961 and was appointed editor in 1964, a position he held until 1974, from which platform he strongly espoused the concept of the free market. Green was among those who encouraged Margaret Thatcher to stand for the Tory party leadership. A keen fly-fisherman on the River Itchen, he died on 19 July 1987 in Winchester.

There can be few children of the middle years of the twentieth century who didn't grow up reading *Adventures of the Little Wooden Horse* (1938), the best-known work by **Ursula Moray Williams** (1911–2006). Ursula was born in Petersfield, by ten minutes the younger of identical sisters. She and her sister Barbara (*d.* 1975) studied together at Winchester College of Art, but while Barbara progressed to the Royal College of Art, Ursula stayed only a year before deciding that writing was the path for her. *Adventures of the Little Wooden Horse*, written while she was expecting her first child, made her name.

One of Britain's first women career journalists, editors and columnists, **Anne Scott-James, Lady Lancaster** (1913–2009) grew up in London and worked successively for *Vogue*, *Picture Post* and *Harper's Bazaar*. Scott-James was appointed women's editor of the *Sunday Express* in 1953, from which position she helped shape the way women's interests were handled generally by the national press. Towards the end of her life, she moved to Sutton Manor nursing home in Sutton Scotney, near Winchester, and died at the Royal Hampshire County Hospital, Winchester, on 13 May 2009. Her son is Max Hastings, former editor-in-chief of *The Daily Telegraph*.

The Henry Root Letters, published in 1980, were a huge hit, a series of spoof letters to leading personalities, printed alongside their replies. Their author was **William Donaldson** (1935–2005), writer, impresario and former Winchester College student. Tragically, Winchester was to impact on Donaldson's life in a more sombre way too. His mother was killed in a car crash near Winchester in 1955; his father didn't recover from his loss and died less than two years later. Donaldson's other works include the semi-fictional memoir *From Winchester to This* (1997).

The award-winning British travel writer and novelist **Jonathan Raban** (*b.* 14 June 1942), who has lived in Seattle since 1990, attended Peter Symonds School in Winchester in the 1950s. His works include *Arabia Through the Looking Glass* (1979), *Old Glory: An American Voyage* (1981), *Coasting* (1986), *God, Man and Mrs Thatcher* (1989), *Passage to Juneau* (1999), *Surveillance* (2006) and *Driving Home: An American Journey* (2011).

Award-winning British novelist, poet and dramatist **Julia Darling** (1956–2005) was born in College Street, Winchester, the daughter of a science teacher at Winchester College. Growing up in the house in which Jane Austen died, Darling was educated at Winchester County High School for Girls. She moved to the north-east in 1980 where she pursued her career as a writer. *Small Beauties* (1988) was her first collection of poems, followed by plays including *Doughnuts Like Fanny's* (2002). She wrote extensively and movingly about her experiences of cancer, from which she died on 13 April 2005.

Contemporary Scottish poet, critic and literary journalist **Lachlan Mackinnon** (*b.* 1956) was born in Aberdeen and educated at Charterhouse and Christ Church College, Oxford. He taught English at Winchester College until early retirement in 2011. His first collection *Monterey Cypress* was published in 1988. His critical works include *Shakespeare the Aesthete: An Exploration of Literary Theory* (1988).

Santa Montefiore has written novels including *Last Voyage of the Valentina* (2005), *The Gypsy Madonna* (2006), *The French Gardener* (2008) and *The Woman from Paris* (2013). The sister of Tara Palmer-Tomkinson, she was born in Winchester on 2 February 1970.

Saving the Cathedral

It is difficult to think of anyone to whom Winchester owes a greater debt than **William Walker** (1869–1918), the man who single-handedly saved the cathedral when it faced the worst crisis in its 900-year history.

Huge cracks started to appear in the walls in the early years of the twentieth century; masonry started to tumble. The whole cathedral, it seemed, was sinking – a victim of the high water table and the peaty soil beneath it. The building needed to be underpinned urgently, and when early efforts failed, Walker, a deep-sea diver, was brought in on a rescue mission as remarkable as any of the fanciful myths – St Swithun's broken eggs, round tables *et al.* – which have grown up around the city. Almost every day for six years, working two four-hour shifts a day, Walker worked underwater, placing bags of concrete exactly where the subsiding cathedral needed them most. Up to 150 other workmen were involved, but the hero was Walker who painstakingly sealed the cathedral fifteen to twenty feet below the surface. The feat is mind-boggling: single-handedly, he slipped modern foundations under a Norman cathedral.

Walker finished his work in 1911, and on St Swithun's day 1912, the cathedral held a service of national thanksgiving to mark its salvation. Walker received honourable mention and indeed honours, but surely he deserved rather better than the fate which life then dealt him. Walker fell victim to Spanish flu and died of pneumonia on 30 October 1918 – one of as many as 100 million deaths worldwide in an epidemic which killed more people in a year than the Black Death killed in a century.

Remarkably, it wasn't until 1964 that Winchester Cathedral decided he warranted a statue. Unfortunately, when the statue was unveiled, it emerged that it wasn't of Walker at all, thanks to a confusion over photographs. The mistake has since been corrected.

Military Men and Women
of Distinction

From the city's earliest days, valour has been a Winchester virtue, to which the city's barracks have added the city's military tradition. Many servicemen and women have made Winchester their home in later life.

The military career of **Sir Cecil James East** (1837–1908) spanned much of the nineteenth-century military history of our country. Born at Herne Hill, Surrey, he was present at the siege and fall of Sevastopol, served during the Indian Mutiny in 1857 and was deputy adjutant and quartermaster-general throughout the latter part of the Anglo-Zulu War. East fought during the Third Anglo-Burmese War in 1886–1887 and then returned to India before being appointed governor of the Royal Military College, Sandhurst (1893–1898). He retired to Fairhaven, Winchester, where he lived the last ten years of his life.

Plymouth-born naval officer **Sir Osmond de Beauvoir Brock** (1869–1947) was promoted to rear-admiral in 1915 and served as chief of staff to Admiral David Beatty, commander-in-chief of the Grand Fleet. After World War One, he served as deputy chief of the naval staff at the Admiralty and became commander-in-chief of the Mediterranean Fleet. He was promoted to admiral in July 1924 and commander-in-chief, Portsmouth, in 1926. In 1929 he was promoted to admiral of the fleet and retired in 1934. He died at his home, St Anns, Links Road, Winchester, on 14 October 1947.

Irish-born naval officer **Sir Frederic Charles Dreyer** (1878–1956) was an ambitious man, the author in 1900 of *How to Get a First Class in Seamanship*. Gunnery became his speciality, and in 1907 he was an experimental gunnery officer on *Dreadnought's* first cruise, later advising the Home Fleet on their gunnery training. Dreyer in addition worked on a number of gunnery inventions, including – with his brother – a device for obtaining range rates from a plot of ranges against time. He also worked on new and effective armour-piercing shell for the Grand Fleet. Dreyer retired in 1939 and died at his home, Freelands, St Cross, Winchester.

Archibald Percival Wavell, first Earl Wavell, (1883–1950) commanded the British Army forces in North Africa and the Middle East during World War Two. Promoted to field marshal in January 1943, he was appointed Governor-General and Viceroy of India later that year. Born in Colchester, Wavell was educated at Winchester College. In 1947 he was created Earl Wavell with the additional title of Viscount Keren of Eritrea and Winchester. Following his death, his body lay in the chapel of St John at the Tower before a funeral service at Westminster Abbey where the bearer party were formed by men of his regiment, the Black Watch. He was laid to rest in the Chantry Close of his old school at Winchester.

RAF officer **Richard Charles Montagu Pink** (1888–1932) seemed destined for the highest office until his life was tragically cut short by cancer. Pink was born at Hyde Cottage, Hyde Street, Winchester. Initially he served in the Royal Navy before transferring to the Royal Naval Air Service at the start of World War One. When the Royal Air Force was created on 1 April 1918, Pink transferred again, serving in Egypt and then in India with distinction. Back in England, in July 1931 he was appointed air commodore. Higher office beckoned, but less than a year later, he was dead, succumbing to cancer on 7 March 1932.

A key figure in the creation and early years of the Women's Royal Air Force, **Dame (Mary) Henrietta**

Barnett (1905–1985) was born at Glasnevin, Barnes Close, Winchester. She rose to become officer-in-charge of the Women's Auxiliary Air Force at the Air Ministry during the early years of World War Two. After the war, she was part of the transition which saw the WAAF become a permanent, enlisted service and eventually the Women's Royal Air Force. When the WRAF came into being on 1 February 1949, Barnett was one of its two deputy directors, later becoming director of the WRAF with the acting rank of air commandant.

Sir James Alfred (Jack) Easton (1908–1990) was born in Winchester and educated at the city's Peter Symonds School. He joined the RAF and after a number of postings returned to the UK. Early in World War Two, he joined the intelligence directorate of the Air Ministry where his particular responsibility was to develop a new section aimed at securing technical intelligence from crashed German aircraft. Easton was also involved in efforts to counter the threat of the V1 flying bomb and the V2 rockets. In 1958, Easton was appointed British consul-general in Detroit, Michigan, where he remained until his death in 1990.

A Horticultural Great

Horticulturist **Sir Harold George Hillier** (1905–1985) was born into the family nursery business, but he took it to new heights, giving Hampshire and the world the Sir Harold Hillier Gardens, at Jermyns Lane, Romsey, nine miles from Winchester.

Hillier was born in Romsey Road, Winchester and attended the city's Peter Symonds School before joining Hillier Nurseries in 1921. He became head of the firm on his father's death in 1944 and travelled widely, deepening his knowledge and expanding his ever-growing plant collection. His aim, he said, was 'to create as attractively as possible as great a collection of plants as I was able to add to those already collected by my father and grandfather'.

The gardens are his greatest contribution to the field of conservation. To secure their future in 1977, he made them a charitable trust, with Hampshire

County Council the sole trustee. The gardens grow 11,000 different types of plants and are recognised by a Grade II listing in English Heritage's Register of Parks and Gardens of Special Historic Interest.

WINCHESTER TIMES

A Glimpse of Winchester
in the 1920s

*With all its peaceful charms, Winchester is
not a dull or lifeless town. The age of motors
has made it not only a place of rest and
pilgrimage, but also a centre for healthy
pleasure. The winter gaieties include three
Hunt balls and a County ball, which are held
in the spacious Guildhall.*

CITY GUIDE (1929)

In the opening weeks of World War One, no fewer
than 30,000 volunteers passed through Winchester
on their way to serve with the King's Royal Rifle Corps
and the Rifle Brigade. A decade later, Winchester
was a city revelling in a new era of peace, full of all
the optimism of the 'roaring twenties' – as a glance
at the 1929 *City Guide* will show.

Flick through the pages, and within moments you want to be there, at that moment – a time when you could enjoy the 'good cuisine, moderate charges, ales, wines, spirits and cigars' on offer at either of the slightly-unfortunately named Dumpers Restaurants in the High Street or Jewry Street, back in the days when the street names were written High-st and Jewry-st. Nearby you could drop into Hunt & Co, the Old Winchester Pharmacy, trusting their promises that their prescriptions are 'accurately prepared with the purest drugs and chemicals'. T A Brown & Son's will meet your clothing needs, offering 'gowns, costumes, millinery, coats, furs, gloves, hosiery, lingerie, linens, men's wear', while the *Hampshire Chronicle* promises itself as 'a splendid medium for advertisements.'

At the Winchester Water & Gas Works, you can enjoy a little foretaste of the future: 'the clean constant flame that provides sun-warmth, cooks your food, heats water, washes and irons clothes and gives you freedom from uncertainty and worry.' For one-stop shopping you can drop in at the Mercantile Furnishing Stores, 'the store where under one roof you shop in comfort and obtain all your requirements with the certainty of getting the Best Value'. After that, you'll almost certainly need a little refreshment at the Georgian Pantry in Great Minster Street, where the specialities are 'biscuits, macaroons, orange cake and opera caramels' before dropping in at John Kaines, 'pork purveyor and provision merchant', to get something for supper.

WINCHESTER CULTURE

Winchester Reaches
for the Stars

Oscar winners, movie moguls, presenters and entertainers have all enjoyed Winchester associations as the showbiz world expanded massively in the twentieth and twenty-first centuries.

J. Arthur Rank (1888–1972) was a British industrialist who became one of the world's most significant producers of motion pictures. He began by making religious films, before turning to commercial work where he showed a Midas touch. By 1941, Rank controlled two of the three largest cinema chains in Great Britain. The J. Arthur Rank company dominated British film production during the late 1940s and 1950s. During the war, Rank did much to maintain the patriotic spirit which kept the country going, making films including *In Which We Serve* (1942) and *Henry V* (1944).

In the early 1930s, Rank rented Tichborne Park, near Alresford, for shooting game before buying Sutton Manor, in Sutton Scotney just north of Winchester, where he accumulated a 14,000 acre estate. He was created Baron Rank of Sutton Scotney in 1957 and died in the Royal Hampshire County Hospital, Winchester, on 29 March 1972. Rank was buried at Sutton Scotney. Sutton Manor is now a private nursing home.

A maker of groundbreaking television documentaries, **Michael Gill** (1923–2005) is remembered particularly for his work on *Civilisation: A Personal View* by Kenneth Clark (1969) and *Alistair Cooke's America* (1973). Other programmes he worked on included the arts series *Monitor* with Huw Wheldon and *Royal Heritage* (1976) to mark the Queen's Silver Jubilee. He was born at The Firs, Weeke Hill, Winchester.

Cyril Nicholas Henty-Dodd (1935–2009), better known by his stage name **Simon Dee**, was once one of the most familiar names in British light entertainment. He was Radio Caroline's first pirate DJ in 1964; he also hosted *Simon's Scene* for Radio Luxembourg and appeared on ITV's *Ready, Steady, Go!* He was an early presenter on BBC 1's *Top of the Pops*, but struck gold with his twice-weekly, early-evening chat show *Dee Time* on the BBC. With its famous catchphrase 'It's Siiiiiiiiimon Dee', it attracted the biggest names from the 1960s as its guests and audiences of up to ten million viewers. He lived the last fifteen years of his life in Winchester where he died at the Royal Hampshire County Hospital on 29 August 2009.

Christopher Cazenove's screen appearances include *There's a Girl in My Soup* (1970), *Duchess of Duke Street* (1976–1977), *Zulu Dawn* (1979), *Eye of the Needle* (1981), *Heat and Dust* (1983) and *A Knight's Tale* (2001). On stage, he starred as Henry Higgins in both British and American productions of *My*

Fair Lady from 2005 to 2008. He was born on 17 December 1943 in Winchester and died in London on 7 April 2010.

Mark Easton (*b.* 12 March 1959) is the Home Editor for BBC News. He was born in Scotland, but the family moved to Winchester when he was ten, and he attended Peter Symonds Grammar School.

A professional quizzer since 2002, **Kevin Ashman** (*b.* 2 November 1959) is one of the world's most successful quiz players. His first success was on the show *Fifteen to One*; he went on to be crowned *Brain of Britain* and then *Brain of Brains*, in which Brains of Britain went head to head. He has also enjoyed success on *Sale of the Century*, *Screen Test* and *The Great British Quiz*. He has been an *Egghead* on the BBC quiz show since 2003. Born and bred in Winchester, Ashman counts Waterstones in Winchester among his favourite haunts.

On 19 October 2007, Oscar-winning actor **Colin Firth** (*b*. 10 September 1960) was awarded an honorary degree by the University of Winchester, recognition not just of his acting achievements, but also his strong links with the city. Firth was born in Grayshott, Hampshire, to parents who both taught at King Alfred's College, Winchester (now the University of Winchester). Firth attended the Montgomery of Alamein Secondary School (now Kings' School) in Winchester and then Barton Peveril Sixth Form College in Eastleigh. In 1995, he became a household name thanks to his portrayal of Mr Darcy in the television adaptation of Jane Austen's *Pride and Prejudice*. His films include *Bridget Jones's Diary* (2001), *Love Actually* (2003), *St Trinian's* (2007), *Mamma Mia!* (2008), and *The King's Speech* (2010), for which he won the Best Actor Oscar.

A household name thanks to his deadpan observations on the miseries of life, comedian **Jack**

Dee (*b.* 24 September 1961) was born in Bromley, Kent. The family moved to Winchester where he attended The Pilgrims' School and Montgomery of Alamein School before taking A-levels at Peter Symonds College. His shows have included *The Jack Dee Show* (1992–1994), *Jack Dee: Live at the Apollo* (2004–2006) and *Lead Balloon* (2006–2011).

Television presenter **Philippa Forrester** was born in Winchester on 20 September 1968. Forrester attended Westgate School in Winchester and also Peter Symonds College. She has worked on shows including *Tomorrow's World*, *The Heaven and Earth Show* and *Robot Wars*.

Rick Adams – also known as DJ Rick – is a television presenter and online radio DJ, who was born in Winchester on 16 October 1971. He has worked for networks including Nickelodeon, Children's BBC,

Bravo and ITV in the UK. He was also a co-presenter on Channel 4's *The Big Breakfast*.

In the tabloids, actress **Isabella Calthorpe** has been labelled the one that got away... from Prince William. He is reported to have pursued her when he briefly broke up with Kate Middleton. Calthorpe was born Isabella Amaryllis Charlotte Anstruther-Gough-Calthorpe in the Royal Hampshire County Hospital at Winchester on 3 March 1980. Her films include *Stage Beauty* (2004), *How to Lose Friends & Alienate People* (2008), *Blooded* (2011) and *Fedz* (2013). Her small-screen credits include *The Inspector Lynley Mysteries* (2006) and the TV miniseries *The Prisoner* (2009).

Ron Howard's Hollywood blockbuster *The Da Vinci Code* (2006), based on Dan Brown's bestselling novel, used Winchester Cathedral among its locations, as did Shekhar Kapur's Elizabeth I epic, *The Golden Age* (2007), starring Cate Blanchett, Clive Owen and Geoffrey Rush.

Winchester returned to the big screen when both Winchester College and Winchester Cathedral were used as one of the many locations for the filming of the cinema version of the stage musical, *Les Misérables* (2012). Winchester College also featured in a TV adaptation of *Goodbye Mr Chips* (2002), starring Martin Clunes as the eponymous schoolmaster.

WINCHESTER CULTURE

Winchester Hat Fair

Every July, Winchester becomes a riot of colour, invention and eccentricity. The **Hat Fair**, Britain's longest running festival of street theatre and outdoor arts, takes its name from the tradition of throwing donations into performers' hats. It takes over the city with a wonderful array of entertainments which bring the streets and the cathedral green to life with a vibrant display of wide-ranging talents.

The fair started life in 1974 as a buskers' festival. It now offers a weekend full of hundreds of performances, still holding good to the principle enshrined in its name. The majority of the performances are free; if you enjoy them, you show your appreciation by whipping out your wallet. Behind it all is the highest and simplest of aims: to provide a welcoming, supportive environment for the country's street performers and so give them the chance to excel.

Political Scandal

Scandal homed in on Winchester when Conservative MP **John Browne** was suspended from the House of Commons in 1990 for failing to declare his business interests. He was deselected by the Conservative Party, but was determined to retain his Winchester seat at the 1992 general election. Browne stood as an Independent Conservative candidate – and fell flat on his face, coming fourth with 30,000 votes fewer than the official Conservative candidate Gerry Malone, a former MP for Aberdeen South, who was duly elected the new MP for Winchester.

However, it wasn't long before things turned sour for **Gerry Malone**. At the 1997 general election, he unexpectedly lost his Winchester seat by two votes to the Liberal Democrat candidate Mark Oaten – a result he promptly challenged. The general election night result was declared void, and a by-election was held, with Malone and Oaten once more contesting the seat. Malone told the world: 'My purpose is to dispel, once and for all, the doubt surrounding the outcome of the election and ensure that the result properly reflects the intentions of voters.'

The voters were happy to oblige. They left Malone in absolutely no doubt whatsoever what their intentions were. Oaten's two-vote majority was turned into a thumping majority of 21,566 – a remarkable 68 per cent of the vote.

But scandals, it seems, like to come in threes. **Mark Oaten** built himself an excellent reputation as a hard-working constituency MP and also won praise as his party's home affairs spokesman. He was clearly a rising star in the Liberal Democrat movement, and it came as no surprise when he announced, in early 2006, that he would stand for the leadership of the Liberal Democrat party. However, Oaten failed to gain sufficient support within the parliamentary party, and nine days later he withdrew from the contest. Just a few days after that, his political career was over. The *News of the World* revealed that he had hired a twenty-three-year-old male prostitute between the summer of 2004 and February 2005. Oaten stood down from Parliament at the 2010 general election.

Royal Moments

Elizabeth II's Golden and Diamond Jubilees in 2002 and 2012 respectively were marked with important new additions to Winchester's stock of public art.

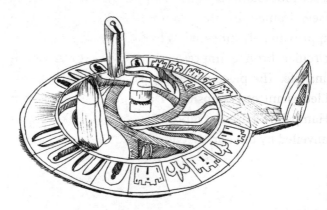

On 21 November 2003, the Queen herself unveiled the **Hampshire Jubilee Sculpture,** close to the Great Hall. Produced by local artist Rachel Fenner, the open-

air sculpture draws inspiration from Winchester's Castle and its Cathedral and also from Hampshire's natural resources to give a sense of Winchester's history and location. A round table is included; arches and arcades underline Winchester's religious importance; and a throne hints at Winchester's royal and episcopal significance.

Inside the Great Hall, the **Diamond Jubilee Bronze** is a six-foot diameter bas-relief portrait of the Queen's face, framed by the Hampshire Rose. Projecting approximately nine inches from its background, the circular bronze impressively conveys both depth and life. The piece was commissioned by the Lord-Lieutenant of Hampshire, Dame Mary Fagan, from Hampshire-based sculptor Vivien Mallock. It was unveiled by the Earl of Wessex on 29 January 2013.

Sticky Ends

Fate deals the cruellest hands. Winchester has not been exempt.

Waltheof, Earl of Northumbria (*c*.1050–1076) was the only English aristocrat to be executed during the reign of William I. A rather more curious distinction is that he apparently continued to recite the Lord's Prayer as his head tumbled to the ground.

A considerable landowner by the time of the Norman Conquest, Waltheof was among the English aristocrats William the Conqueror kept at court. He rebelled, was pardoned, married the king's niece and then apparently rebelled again. William was not impressed, and after a year in confinement Waltheof was executed on St Giles' Hill outside Winchester on 31 May 1076 – which is when the legend began.

Reciting the Lord's Prayer, he had reached 'Lead us not into temptation' as the sword descended. As his head fell, 'But deliver us from evil' was distinctly heard to come from his lips. Or so the story goes…

Kings simply don't come less popular than William II (c.1056 – 2 August 1100), better known as **William Rufus**, the despised son of William I and Matilda. The *Anglo-Saxon Chronicle* records that he was 'hateful to almost all his people and odious to God'. Some historians argue that he really wasn't that bad, that his reputation rests on the portrait painted of him by biased monastic chroniclers who hated him because of his demands on the Church. But such bias aside, it's still difficult to find anything much to commend him. Reaction to his death probably says all that needs to be said about him.

William Rufus' reign came to the most sudden of ends when he was shot dead with an arrow while hunting in the New Forest. The arrow is generally believed to have been fired by Walter Tirel. Whether it was murder or simply an accident will never be known. Plenty of his contemporaries regarded it as an act of God, a just reward for a wicked, ruthless, bellicose king.

His body was offered little respect. His mortal remains were dumped on a cart and trundled twenty miles to Winchester where they were hastily buried beneath the tower at Winchester Cathedral. When the tower collapsed seven years later, again there were plenty prepared to see it as divine disapproval as a rotter once again reaped the rewards of his failings – tyranny, avarice, blasphemy and sodomy, to name just a few, if the Church were to be believed. Adding further insult to arrow-inflicted injury, it seems that his tomb in Winchester Cathedral might not even be his. It is now generally believed more likely that it contains not William I's son, but his grandson, Bishop Henry de Blois.

Sir Walter Raleigh was a man of many distinctions, an aristocrat who was also a poet, a courtier who was also an explorer, a soldier who was also a spy. He even popularised tobacco in this country. None of it, however, saved his life when he stood trial in

Winchester's Great Hall, charged with treason on 17 November 1603.

Raleigh conducted his own defence, winning public sympathy for his composure even when he was sentenced to death. It was very nearly fifteen years later that the sentence was finally carried out, Raleigh meeting his fate in the Old Palace Yard at the Palace of Westminster on 29 October 1618, but not before he had managed a couple of contributions to all future books of quotations.

Looking at the axe which was to behead him, he is said to have mused: 'This is a sharp Medicine, but it is a Physician for all Diseases and Miseries.' His final words, it seems, were: 'Strike, man, strike!' His executioner didn't quite manage it. Raleigh's head fell only at the second blow. It was then placed in a red leather bag and was carried away by his wife, while his body was buried at St Margaret's, Westminster.

Not surprisingly, it was the notorious Judge Jeffreys who was responsible for one of the ghastliest moments in Winchester history when he ordered the execution of **Lady Alice Lisle** for harbouring fugitives after the defeat of the Monmouth Rebellion at the Battle of Sedgemoor.

Lord Chief Justice George Jeffreys travelled from Winchester through the Western Circuit in autumn 1685 on the instructions of James II, trying for treason the rebels and the traitors who had sheltered them. He tried 1,381 people, between 200 and 300 of whom were executed. Some would argue that Jeffreys did not exceed the letter of the law, but few could fail to feel sympathy for the unfortunate Alice Lisle who claimed she had no idea who her refugees were or what they were hiding from.

The court ordered that she should be burnt that very afternoon. Pleas for clemency simply delayed her death and brought an acknowledgement of her standing. Instead of being burnt, she was beheaded – five days later. The sentence was carried out on 2 September 1685 in Winchester market place where the museum now stands. A plaque on the wall of the museum records the grim moment. Lady Alice was 70 years old, the widow of John Lisle, who had been MP for Winchester. Ironically he had been one of the judges at the trial of Charles I.

Thomas Thetcher, or the Hampshire Grenadier, as he is known, has exerted far greater fascination in death than he ever did in life, thanks to the striking inscription on his tombstone just near the entrance to Winchester Cathedral.

In Memory of
THOMAS THETCHER
a Grenadier in the North Reg't
of Hants Militia, who died of a
violent Fever contracted by drinking
Small Beer when hot the 12th of May
1764. Aged 26 Years.

In grateful remembrance of whose universal
good will towards his Comrades, this Stone
is placed here at their expence, as a small
testimony of their regard and concern.
Here sleeps in peace a Hampshire Grenadier,
Who caught his death by drinking cold small Beer
Soldiers be wise from his untimely fall
And when ye're hot drink Strong or none at all.

It seems that the poor chap was a victim of the days when beer was safer to drink than water. Thetcher's misfortune was to drink small beer, in other words a second brewing which had diluted the alcohol and therefore exposed him to the dangers of the water the beer contained. And, for Thomas Thetcher, that was that in this life. A century and a half later, Thetcher's tombstone caught the attention of World War One American soldier Bill Wilson who – perhaps slightly misinterpreting the gravestone – went on to become one of the founders of Alcoholics Anonymous.

James Aitken (1752–1777) was executed on the highest gallows England has ever seen, hanged from the mizzen mast of the *Arethusa*, which had been erected on Portsmouth Common especially for the occasion on a day which attracted crowds some 20,000 strong. To them all, Aitken was better known as **John the Painter**, the man who had declared war on the country's dockyards.

Born in Edinburgh, Aitken drifted south into a life of crime in London. Briefly, he tried to make a new life for himself in Virginia but returned to England, resolved to do his bit for the American revolutionary cause. His aim was to destroy all six of the royal dockyards, starting with Portsmouth and then Bristol. On his arrest, he was taken to Winchester where he was tried in the Great Hall in March

1777. Aitken defended himself, was convicted and condemned to death. At first he continued to deny his guilt, but then had a change of heart and dictated a confession to Winchester's jailor. Local printer J. Wilkes published his admission as *The Life of James Aitken* (1777).

Today 'Fanny Adams' is an expression meaning 'nothing at all' or 'nothing of worth'; in the immediate aftermath of poor Fanny's brutal murder, her name conjured revulsion and horror across the country. Eight-year-old **Fanny Adams** (1859–1867) was playing with her sister in their home town of Alton on Saturday 24 August 1867 when a man approached them and offered them money for sweets. Fanny was then abducted, murdered and dismembered. It took days to recover all the body parts.

Solicitor's clerk Frederick Baker was arrested, committed for trial and taken to Winchester prison. He was convicted at the county assizes, condemned to death and hanged before a crowd thousands strong at 8 a.m. on Christmas Eve 1867, one of the last public executions held in Winchester.

It is thanks to grim naval humour in Portsmouth that Fanny's name lives on. Faced with tins of unappetising-looking mutton, the sailors remarked that the meat was chopped up so much it was actually unrecognisable, rather like sweet Fanny Adams. 'Sweet F A' became service slang for mutton before changing to the current meaning 'nothing of worth'.

Things that Go Bump
in the Night…

Just as you'd expect in a city as old as Winchester, tales of ghosts abound.

Inevitably, a good number centre on the Cathedral and the Cathedral Close. Monks fading to nothing below the knees have been sighted in the building, and a 1957 photograph apparently caught 13 ghostly figures standing in front of the altar.

Outside, a limping monk hobbles around the Cathedral Close, moving surprisingly quickly given his disability. Ghostly chanting in Latin has been heard in the area, and a spectral horseman has been known to gallop straight through walls.

Meanwhile a vengeful beggar woman is apparently back at the Hyde Tavern. The unfortunate wretch pleaded in vain for refuge on a bitterly cold night, but was turned away. She was found frozen to death the next morning. Apparently she still groans in her anguish.

Not far away, the Jolly Farmer inn is said to be haunted by a man hanged nearby for theft. Dubbed Drunk Henry, he specialises in childish mischief-making.

A man in a tricorn hat has apparently been seen to pass through a wall in the Great Hall, while at the former *Hampshire Chronicle* offices, now Zizzi's restaurant, in the High Street, it's the so-called clanking woman who serves up the surprises. One particular sighting in 2001 was of a shadowy mass which floated through a wall. More usually, the clanking woman is heard rather than seen. Her penchant is to rattle chains and/or machinery.

Lady Alice Lisle, so famously executed in the city, can be heard walking along the corridors, with a swish of her silk dress, at her former home Moyles Court, near Ringwood. She is also said to haunt The Eclipse Inn in Winchester where she spent her last night before being publicly beheaded.

A theatre is not a theatre without a ghost, and the Theatre Royal Winchester can boast three at least. Its builder John Simpkins has been known to return, and so too has a lighting operator who was killed in World War One. Another ghost in the theatre is that of a woman vainly waiting for her long-lost lover to come back.

The stories are just as colourful in the Winchester Discovery Centre, formerly the Corn Exchange, next door. Ghostly footsteps have been heard at night, and unearthly arias are said to float up from the basement.

Look back at Winchester's rich and fascinating history, and it is fitting that those songs should still be heard, that the clanking woman should clank and that Drunk Henry should still make merry from beyond the grave.

After all, Winchester has always allowed its past to live and breathe in its everyday present. It's precisely the reason this ancient capital now sits so comfortably in the twenty-first century – and the reason it looks to its future with confidence.

Also in this series:

A CHICHESTER MISCELLANY

978 1 84953 379 9
Hardback
£9.99

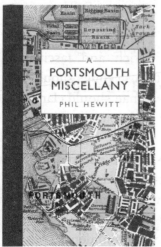

A PORTSMOUTH MISCELLANY

978 1 84953 463 5
Hardback
£9.99

Have you enjoyed this book?
If so, why not write a review on
your favourite website?

If you're interested in finding out more
about our books, find us on Facebook
at **Summersdale Publishers** and follow
us on Twitter at **@Summersdale**.

Thanks very much for buying
this Summersdale book.

www.summersdale.com